D1710893

Building Shelters, Fences and Jumps

Andy Radford

Riding a horse or pony is an immense pleasure, especially over safe obstacles.

Building Shelters, Fences and Jumps

Andy Radford

The Crowood Press

First published in 2004 by
The Crowood Press Ltd
Ramsbury, Marlborough
Wiltshire SN8 2HR

www.crowood.com

British Library Cataloguing-in-Publication Data
A catalogue record for this book is available from the British
Library.

ISBN 1 86126 658 8

Dedication
This book is dedicated to Pat and Jim Radford.

Unless otherwise stated all diagrams and photographs are the
copyright of the author.

Typeset by Carreg Limited, Ross-on-Wye, Herefordshire

Printed and bound in Great Britain by The Cromwell Press,
Trowbridge

CONTENTS

ACKNOWLEDGEMENTS

I would like to thank the following people and organizations for their valued help in putting this book together: first, Martin Roscoe, Ray Parry, Emyr Griffiths, Derek Wellings and Darren Russell for their help and advice on field shelter construction. Also Mary Evans, Natasha Thomas, Charlotte Randall, Sarah Butler, Sarah Stanton, Ewa Jordan, Fred Hart and Aimy McGinty of Daywell Manor for their input into cross-country jump construction. Anne Roberts and Gwynedd Shaw of the Berwyn and Dee branch of the Pony Club; Karen Czora of 'Karen Czora Photography' for her advice on equine photography; Paul, Chris, Abbie and Joanne Gurnett for allowing me to photograph on their land; Laura Tudor on Jester for being excellent photographic subjects and ETC Saw Mills for technical help and sponsorship of materials. And finally, Janet Williams, Jamie and Crisiant Radford.

INTRODUCTION

Although this book is not intended to be a complete answer to every equine structural problem and need (there are certain situations that require expert, hands-on input), the following projects should be enough to keep horse, rider and owner happy for a long time.

Owning equine stock can be both a rewarding and pleasurable experience, and there is no better sight than watching a horse or pony gracefully wander about a paddock. Horses and ponies do have their drawbacks, however, particularly with regard to finance, and the paraphernalia that comes with them can prove very expensive: by 'paraphernalia' I mean the large and small constructions that are required to provide them with comfort, shelter and exercise. These are the essentials – but there are also the costs incurred when owning one of these animals for simply leisure and pleasure: show jumping, cross country, and even hacking around your own back yard can lead to a costly outlay when it comes to building a small jumping course or cross-country fence on your land. The aim of this book is to describe some money-saving techniques that can be employed without in any way compromising the safety of horse and rider.

Based on the most popular aspects of horse or pony ownership, the following chapters will guide you through the basics of building a simple field shelter, a basic show-jumping fence, and some easy, child-friendly cross-country obstacles. Maintenance issues are also covered, such as repairing and building stable doors and erecting a suitable enclosure fence.

Perhaps the most common of all essential equine structures is a horse-proof fence. Although this book covers two styles of enclosure – a universal stock fence and a timber post and rail assembly – it is the latter which is the most suitable. Ideally the equine fence should be kept free of any form of wire and netting. Having said that, in some situations correctly tensioned netting can prove effective for docile animals. There is, nonetheless, a very strong and tangible argument against this style, as the horse or pony could tangle and trap a hoof between the netting's gaps. Considering the fact that many netted fences aren't tensioned properly it is no wonder that equine owners are untrusting of this method. If at all possible, please be advised to install a post and rail.

As with anything that involves the use of tools and the construction of facilities used by people and animals, safety must be a high priority. The chapter devoted to safety issues is important, and in each of the practical chapters, further advice concerning safety in relation to the work in hand is given when necessary.

The safety of horse and rider cannot be emphasized enough. The slightest irregularity on a show jump or entrance to a stable could result in serious injury. These hazards include splinters in timber, damaged hinges with sharp corners or even the smallest of nail ends left as an oversight after a maintenance task. An accident sustained whilst riding could, in turn, injure the rider. It is obvious, then, that when construction work is complete a meticulous, even painstaking search of the site should be carried out. If the task involved dismantling an old wire fence there is every chance that some wire could be buried just under the surface of the ground. Whilst this is not a major problem in the summer, where the ground usually remains hard and compact due to the continual pounding of hooves, in winter, however, this very same action can churn a pasture into a muddy quagmire revealing the danger underneath.

When building a shelter, shed or loosebox, planning permission is an important and sometimes confusing factor, depending on the size and type of the intended structure. Some of the projects described in this book may require permission from a local planning authority, and there is a chapter dedicated to this subject: it explains how to apply for planning authorization, and tells you which facets of the law are taken into consideration when buildings for horse-related activities are contemplated.

One of the subjects that concerns most people is the actual cost of materials and tools. Purchasing the most cost-effective goods from suitable retailers is discussed, as are the relevant tools and equipment. Indeed, no project can be undertaken without adequate tools, and most of the implements used are standard household items that would be used in a garden or as part of an everyday DIY exercise.

CHAPTER 1

GETTING STARTED

Safety

The main consideration in a do-it-your-self enterprise is the welfare of the animal and the people who intend to use the equipment or structure. At no time should safety be taken lightly, as this could turn out to be costly in health, finance and time; thus when erecting any structure, meticulous planning and a diligent approach to the physical work should be common practice. And particularly where equines are concerned, the smallest hazard could well develop into a major problem – it is only too easy to overlook a stray nail lying on the floor, or a loose-fitting panel that threatens to blow off in a gust of wind, yet both are potentially damaging to life and limb. Furthermore, bearing in mind the high quantity of fixings required, even for lightweight tasks, a protruding nail-point or sharp-ended bolt may be easily missed, and it is this sort of common oversight that all too frequently takes its toll on ponies, horses, children and adults. It is important to realize that horses have an uncanny knack of finding the weak points in any structure, whether it is driven into the ground or attached to a wall, and left unrepaired, these could become an accident waiting to happen.

Before you begin any building work, the first, and probably the single most important issue, is knowing the animal. It is a waste of time installing a new hayrack, for example, if you know the pony has a reputation for messing about, because in all probability it will endeavour to pull all its forage onto the ground, and will then 'play' with the hayrack. This could lead to serious injury if it happens to break the rack or, worse still, gets stuck in it overnight.

Tool Safety

Working with hand tools poses the greater risk to the user, although an unattended device will become a hazard to a pony if it is using the paddock you are working in. This is true for all tools. In fact, learning how to use tools in the proper manner can enhance the enjoyment of the work and speed up the job with a minimum of fuss and risk. Electrical power tools make light work of heavy jobs, and some of the projects described later rely on their use. As most of the projects in this book can be built outside, attention must be paid to the safety advice that comes with the items when they are purchased. This is all down to common-sense work practices: in damp or wet conditions they must not be used; always use a circuit breaker; and uncoil extension cables to their full extent, and make sure that they, too, have an integrated circuit breaker. A common, sometimes fatal injury is electrocution, and steps must be taken to avoid this. Check the cables of all power tools for splits on the outer insulating sheaths and, needless to say, if the cables are worn, either discard or repair the tool.

Using power tools around horses and ponies is not recommended, and the animals should be moved to a safe, fenced-off area away from the work site. On no account carry out maintenance work in an enclosed space with an equine, as sudden or continuous noise may scare it, cables can be trodden on, and stray screws or nails could cause severe injury. Again, move the animal to a safe area – and preferably not the stable next door if this can be avoided. When working in a field you should erect a temporary enclosure well away from the work site; this can be done simply with an electric fence.

Another major hazard associated with electrical tools is fire. When using drills or power saws in a stable block, the surrounding area must be clear of dry hay and bedding. Adequate fire precautions should be implemented before work commences, and some means to control fire should be available as a matter of health and safety.

Hand tools such as saws and screwdrivers are to be treated with respect; it is very easy for the blade to slip and cut through a hand or finger. Believe it or not there is a correct way to hold these tools: it is called the 'forefinger-thumb' principle, and is more or less the same way that one grips a pen for writing. The forefinger-thumb technique allows the operator to use a tool with the best stability possible. Hammers are another common cause of injury, a misdirected blow can often result in a bruised or broken finger or hand.

Improper use of the larger tools such as spades, crowbars and fencing mauls can turn out to be fatal, and knowing how to use and store them safely is essential. Avoid lifting them above head height, and never place them upright when not in use, as an animal or human passer-by could unwittingly walk into them. Find a safe area close to the work site and away from any public right of way, and inform other people of their exact position.

Personal Safety

Just as tool safety is a necessary work ethic, personal safety should be regarded equally seriously. Never undertake any practical work without basic health and safety equipment. A first-aid kit (and knowing how to use it correctly, of course) is probably the most important piece of equipment you should carry with you, but basic work clothes such as leather safety gloves and steel toe-capped footwear

---

Common Injuries Associated with Bad Working Practices

- Gashed or bruised feet as a result of misusing a spade, crowbar, mattock or pick. Severed toes and head injuries are also common with these tools
- Minor and/or severe cuts due to misuse of saws, small fencing tools and other sharp-ended items
- Minor and/or severe wounds from splinters from wooden building materials such as fencing rails and stakes
- Stab wounds from screwdrivers, chisels and crowbars
- Head injury, maybe fatal, as a result of misusing sledgehammer and fencing maul tools

should be worn at all times. Steel toe-caps are especially important.

If you are working in a confined space with a horse, carrying out quick, simple routine tasks, and there really is no alternative accommodation for the animal, be extremely cautious. Use manual drills and saws instead of their electrical alternatives, and always have an assistant to restrain and soothe the horse, away from the place of work; in fact it would be preferable for the assistant to take it out for a walk 'in hand', if possible, instead of allowing it to remain near the work site.

Performing tasks in the open air brings further dangers: for example, heat stroke, hypothermia and fatigue can all sneak up and catch us unaware. Adequate clothing, high-energy foods, warm or cold drinks (depending on the conditions) and regular breaks are as essential as the first-aid kit mentioned above. Moreover, if the place where you are working is remote, always inform someone of your exact location and estimated finishing time before you begin your work; then if something untoward should occur, they will notice your non-return and would come to your assistance sooner rather than later. Mobile phones have revolutionized safety procedures in the countryside; nevertheless, some forest or mountain regions have reception blindspots, resulting in your cell phone not working effectively.

Equine Safety

Many injuries incurred by equines are quite devastating, sometimes so much so that they have to be destroyed. It is up to the owners or the people working on site (depending who is carrying out the job) to make sure that the area is kept free from potential hazards, particularly as the

---

Common Equine Injuries Due to Bad Working Practices

- A stray nail dropped in the stable or an untrimmed piece of timber could cause a puncture wound in the foot; this could well entail a hefty vet's bill and the animal being out of action for a long time
- An unfilled posthole may cause a broken limb, with potentially dire consequences, the worst scenario being euthanasia of the horse or pony
- Even simply leaving your lunch box in a prominent place could cause a serious digestive disorder if the animal gained access to its contents

---

majority of injuries can be related to bad working practices or absent-mindedness.

Equines also put themselves at risk due to their ingrained 'fright or flight' behaviour when startled, so it is important that people working in their vicinity understand that they will often bolt when startled by a sudden loud noise. In this context it is therefore important to avoid needlessly scaring horses, causing them to run blindly around a field, or to pull back suddenly on a tie rope.

It is also imperative that you warn people as to when you are about to begin hammering or drilling. It would not be conducive to a good schooling session if the horse took off across the manège bucking because a colleague or contractor had picked that precise moment to board up the nearby barn. That would certainly compromise relationships with other horse owners!

Needless to say, unlike most domesticated pets, equines are more prone to injury, and great care must be taken to protect them from harm.

Purchasing Tools and Materials

Of all the domesticated grazing animals, horses and ponies are generally responsible for any damage caused to fences and stabling, largely because they are wilful, intelligent and very strong. Purchasing weak materials or using second-hand goods rarely produces the right results, and a consequence of this is an expensive, laborious maintenance routine. Equines, if hungry, will force themselves through seemingly strong enclosures in an attempt to eat the grass on the other side. In the long run it therefore pays to install strong new timber (and maybe also to review the animal's feeding régime, taking expert advice where necessary). Money well spent now will benefit both the animal and your finances, in that there will be less need for constant maintenance. As a last resort, second-hand products may work if they are in extremely good condition – though in my experience this is very rarely the case.

Choosing the most cost-effective retailer is critical. Unlike other goods, where the price tends to be about the same no matter what shop you look into, the charge for timber produce can vary considerably. Although high-street DIY outlets tend to stock small amounts of agricultural hardware, their range of goods is usually limited to a few fencing stakes, rails, and probably a small choice of wire netting. Most of their floor space caters for the home and garden market, and as a consequence of this, their stock-fencing products tend to be sold at a higher-than-usual price (in my experience, at least).

The same may be said about sectional buildings such as looseboxes: again, the DIY stores' product lines mainly cater for garden sheds, garages, conservatories, rabbit hutches and dog kennels. They do, nonetheless, offer a great range of sundry items such as nails and screws, and can sell you almost any work tool available, apart from specialized fencing devices such as wire strainers (although they may be able to order them). Where metalwork for equestrian buildings is concerned, the only items you might not find in a DIY shop are kick-bolts for stable doors and jump cups for show jumps.

In a large agricultural suppliers' store, such as a Farmers' Union Co-op, you will find almost anything you need for the equine hobby, from fencing goods (including electrical enclosures) and looseboxes, to kick-bolts and jump cups. Fencing tools can be purchased 'off the shelf', as can fencing staples and metal rings for tying a horse.

Farmers' co-ops may be able to supply the widest choice of merchandise, but it is the dedicated agricultural fencing retailers that still offer value for money when it comes to shopping for fencing wares. The prime outlets are sawmills with their own retail premises: not only can they offer all the enclosure requirements you will possibly ever need, but most of them have extended their range to include large equine buildings and other livestock-related constructions – sometimes built to your own specifications. And because they cater for this market you will invariably find an extensive range of sundries stacked on their shelves, probably at the best prices, too.

CHAPTER 2

BASIC REQUIREMENTS

The point of this chapter is to give you some idea of the basic structures you will need before you consider buying a pony or accepting one on loan. The practical instructions for the various buildings mentioned here are discussed in greater detail in the subsequent chapters. (I feel it is wise to mention at this point that equine husbandry is not the subject of this book, and I would strongly recommend that you seek expert advice and tuition before you take on the responsibility of owning and caring for a horse or pony.)

Where to Keep Your Pony

Apart from food and water, a horse or pony requires certain practical features in its husbandry that are important to its well-being, and will enhance the time it lives with you. Before you even think of buying or accepting an animal on loan, you should consider very carefully where it will graze and live. If you are lucky enough to own, or can rent, a small piece of land of about one to two acres, then your first problem, of where to keep it, has been solved. Most equines can live quite happily out of doors in all but the worst weather conditions.

Suitable Fencing

The second factor to consider is the type and condition of the boundary fencing. Equines can destroy even a reasonably strong construction, a recently installed fence being no exception. If the enclosure was used in the past for sheep or cattle, then the existing fence is most likely to be a post and wire affair, which is certainly not ideal for a horse; nevertheless, if the wire has been correctly tensioned it may be all right until a fence of alternative materials can be constructed. An old post-and-rail fence will inevitably have many weak points, and these will become only too apparent should the animal keep breaking through to the other side. Furthermore, an old fence may well be full of potentially injurious hazards such as sharp fragments of metal and barbed wire – a situation that does not really guarantee an ideal beginning to a happy relationship with your new companion.

When inspecting a fence to assess whether it will contain a horse effectively, the first thing you should look at is the height. An animal that is more than 12h.h. should be contained by a structure of around 4ft (1.2m) high, and some large horses may require something taller, of around 6ft (1.8m); but this depends on whether the animal has a quiet personality, or has Houdini-like tendencies. Provided all its needs are met, a docile equine will quite happily graze behind a fence of 4ft (1.2m) for most of the time.

Next to consider are the materials to make the fence stock-proof. As previously discussed, wire netting is not an ideal option, especially if it is old. Similarly, fencing rails should be free from wood-rot and splits, and weak nails will soon give way if the rails are pushed against or leaned on. Fencing posts and stakes should be checked for breakage and also wood-rot; in particular look for decay at ground level, as it is this part of the timber that will always receive the most moisture. A rotten post will snap when forced, and some will probably be broken already.

If the fence has been repaired in the past, which is quite likely, there may be evidence of old postholes: these should be filled with soil or tightly packed with sand at the earliest possible opportunity.

Ponies safely secured behind a post-and-rail fence. These posts are actually full round and pointed, but the fact that they were knocked in with a tractor's post slammer means they were pushed to optimum depth. As such they are strong.

It is also quite common to find broken-off posts still embedded in the ground, and these should be removed quickly because they pose a significant hazard. There may be coils of old wire tangled in the pasture, and this should also be pulled out and cleared away as it, too, poses a considerable risk to humans and livestock.

Access Points

Suitable access points are another crucial consideration. A battered gate is best replaced by a new one of the requisite size: field gates should be at least 5–6ft (1.5–1.8m) wide, but if vehicle access is required, then the smallest size you should really contemplate is 8ft (2.4m); this will make negotiating the entrance much easier when the ground is wet and muddy.

In the same way as you checked the fence posts, inspect the gate hangers or stoops for weakness at ground level, and replace them if they are worn. If the existing gate's furniture is galvanized, it can be cleaned with oil and re-used. The older, black-japanned versions are more prone to rust and may have outlived their working ability; in this case they arc best replaced by galvanized hinges, hangers and catches.

The Field Shelter

A suitable enclosure is not entirely complete without some sort of shelter from the elements. During the summer months mature trees will offer shade and a measure of cover in a torrential downpour, but in the winter this protection will disappear as fast as the canopies fall. A permanent alternative is a simple three-sided (or open-plan) field shelter. This can be easily installed, and all the materials purchased off the shelf from an agricultural supplier or sawmill.

Where to situate it in the paddock depends on the lie of the land. If the ground slopes, it should be built on the highest suitable point, otherwise it may become a water- and mud-trap as rainwater washes down the hillside. Equally it should not be in an exposed location, and the open side should face away from the prevailing winds. It is also important to ensure there is no risk of a horse being trapped between the field shelter and the boundary fence; this is particularly important where several animals are turned out together and bullying may be an issue.

Lastly, depending on its size, a field shelter may need planning permission. This is explained in Chapter 4.

Stabling

With the boundary fencing now planned and the construction of a field shelter well in hand, the next feature to think about is some form of secure accommodation. Having a stable can be of significant advantage in several situations: for example, in adverse weather conditions, when preparing for a competition, or when nursing a sick horse. If you don't know how big a stable should be for your particular animal, seek expert advice before commencing work.

Converting an Existing Building

Perhaps you own an existing building that might be easy to customize. Refitting a large garage, for example, might produce the desired result if you remove the existing doors and replace them with a timber-framed front. You will also have to replace any glass windows, then reconstruct the entire front section with timber or brick, and put in suitable Dutch-style stable doors. From the safety viewpoint it is important to mention that many garages have electrical wiring, and it is essential to remove any wall sockets, light switches and cabling that is within the animal's reach. Ideally you should ask a qualified electrician to remove the supply, only leaving a power point for a single light with a waterproof switch connected somewhere outside.

Another appropriate building could be an existing large garden shed, if it is in a good state of repair. Structurally, however, it would require an extensive refurbishment to make it strong enough to accommodate a pony or horse. Like the garage, electrical wiring will have to be removed, and glass windows taken out. If the shed walls are built of wood, they will almost certainly have to be strengthened, otherwise the animal could injure itself by kicking through them. This can be achieved by adding an internal wall of 1.5–2in (3.8–5cm) plyboard. The doorway will also have to be widened, and as a consequence probably the entrance area, too. If the shed has a timber floor it will be essential to replace it with concrete.

Having said all this, sometimes this sort of conversion is simply not cost-effective; for example, my garden shed sits on six brick pillars and is raised 18in (45cm) off the ground, and the work involved to change it to equine use would be too extensive to contemplate – I would have to dismantle the structure and rebuild it at ground level.

When converting existing buildings it is important to consider the issue of ventilation. Poorly ventilated buildings result in poor air quality, and a build-up of dust, bacteria and ammonia, and exposure to these conditions can predispose a horse to respiratory ailments. Attention should also be given to drainage, to prevent the accumulation of urine on the floor, and to lighting and outlook – most horses like to be able to see what is going on around them, and a horse should never be kept in darkness.

Building a New Loosebox

An alternative to conversion is to build a loosebox using individual sections of new, treated timber. This will involve precise planning and thought, as you will need to know the correct amounts and sizes of materials to purchase; the list will be comprehensive, and will include every single screw, nail and bolt. You will also need to ascertain the quantity of wood needed for the inner and outer walls, for the main frame of the dwelling, and for the roofing and doors. Each stable door will require a complete set of metalwork, and possibly an anti crib-biting barrier (crib-biting is when a horse or pony chews the top of fencing rails or doors).

The loosebox will have to sit on an adequate concrete foundation, so the budget must provide for this – and if you don't fancy digging out the foundation yourself, you will have to hire a mini excavator and driver. You will also have to include the hire of a concrete mixer, aggregates for the base of the foundation and, of course, materials for the concrete mixture itself.

If mixing concrete isn't your forte, many companies can deliver a *ready-mix* solution that is poured straight into the trench direct from their lorry.

The Purpose-Made Loosebox

The whole exercise of building a new loosebox could turn out to be an expensive, frustrating headache as compared to installing a purpose-made loosebox that comes in kit form, especially if you find you are obliged to make regular trips back to the retailer because of mistakes in your calculations. The advantage in buying one of these sectional buildings is that it comes with everything you need, except the materials for a foundation and the electrical supply. All *you* will need to supply are the correct dimensions; then it is the retailer's responsibility to estimate and sell you the correct quantities.

Providing a Water Supply

With the planning for the loosebox complete, the next task should be to provide an adequate water supply. The installation of an outside tap close to the stable could involve major plumbing work, which is all well and good as long as your budget can cope with it. A cheap and easy alternative is to install an outside tap against the external wall of your house, connecting it to existing pipework; you can then run a garden hose to the stable. Furthermore, most fittings nowadays come with units that can clamp to existing pipework without the need for solder. In fact the hardest part of the job will be to punch a hole through the wall to attach the fittings; but with a decent masonry bit, a fairly powerful hammer drill, a lump hammer and a sharp cold chisel or bolster chisel, this should be relatively easy to do. The only drawback with this idea is that tap and hose will freeze during cold spells.

Storage Space

As well as secure stabling, a dry area to store feed and bedding would be an advantage. For reasons of safety this should be sited some distance away from human habitation and equine dwellings. Dry bedding and forage is a serious fire risk – as if you need to be reminded – and once alight, even a relatively small stack of hay will rapidly become an inferno. For this reason you should avoid placing it near to any public right of way, or to the main access points to your land. Arson attacks on agricultural buildings are very common, and every possible step should be taken to make life difficult for these criminals. We store our hay in an old polytunnel, hidden from the public's gaze and away from the stable, and so far it has proved an effective system. Our local country park has suffered two such attacks in recent years, the first one destroying a field shelter and straw, and the second actually killing livestock.

Constructing a Feed Store

A feed store can be constructed using a similar method to the field shelter, but with four walls and a door. There is no structural need to lay a concrete foundation, although some form of flooring would be an advantage in preventing too much damage from vermin and damp.

Old pallets have three distinct advantages in this context: firstly, they are easy to come by, and relatively cheap to purchase; secondly, they make ideal flooring; and lastly, because they are slatted, with the surface area raised off the floor by default, air can circulate underneath, thus protecting hay and straw from mould and fungus.

Dried food mixtures can be stored in metal containers to thwart rodent attacks; old-style cylindrical dustbins are ideal for this job, though purpose-made feed bins may be purchased from farm suppliers.

The Tack Room

As far as equine welfare is concerned, perhaps the least important building is a tack store, where saddles, bridles and other equine paraphernalia can be made secure. Such a store can be purchased as an extension to the purpose-made sectional loosebox described earlier, with the same consumer advantages. Tack, as we all know, is very expensive, so the decision not to keep it in your own home must not be made lightly. Personally, I prefer to keep our pony tack within the security of our cottage. I feel this is the best way of protecting it from the criminal element, and of course brings it under our household insurance policy.

Organizing the Muck Heap

Composting is the next issue to tackle, since an inevitable consequence of looking after equines is the enormous quantity of muck they create. You will have no choice but to set aside an area of your land for the sole purpose of storing it until it can be used for something else. This strenuous daily exercise can be made easier by siting the heap in an easily accessible position some distance from the stable. If it is positioned too close to the loosebox, then the animal will be plagued by flies during the summer months; and storing muck in the vicinity of human dwellings is also not a good idea, for the same reason.

A point worth mentioning here is that horse muck, as with all biodegradable matter, will begin to break down wooden panels if it is piled up against timber outbuildings in substantial quantities. You could if you wished have an area of hard standing surrounded on three sides by a wall, to contain the muck until it is collected.

Laying Hard Standing

A useful option, although not entirely necessary, to the ground surrounding heavily used outbuildings is some form of hard standing to help resist erosion. It is not much fun to have to wade through mud, particularly on dark winter evenings. The best surface to keep clean is concrete, although limestone hardcore will help to reduce a future erosion problem. Avoid a surface of sharp stones, which could well cause lameness.

Building and Siting Jumps

With the hard planning work now out of the way, you can think about the leisure aspects of owning a pony. Horses and ponies are not just beautiful ornaments to look at and admire whilst you are leaning on a fence: an immense amount of pleasure can be gained from riding them. Whilst owning your own show jumps or cross-country fences is gratifying, being able to make them yourself is a bonus. In fact, building them is not as difficult as it sounds, and all that is required is a little knowledge of woodwork, and an ability to work with an element of common sense, safe practice, and prior thought for the animal's welfare whilst using them.

The chapter on building jumps will explain their construction in more detail, but before you even think of installing them in your paddock you must be sure that the ground is free of dangerous obstructions, and preferably on not too much of a gradient. Also important is the landing area after each jump: it should be free of tussocks, hillocks or divots, which could cause serious injury, and it should be long enough to allow the animal to land, put in a few comfortable strides, and turn. If none of the latter can be guaranteed, then I would suggest not pursuing the project any further.

Show jumps are slightly different because, unlike a lot of cross-country fences, which are permanent fixtures, they are generally of lighter construction and can be moved to a safer area. Again, if your land has too many hazardous landing areas then it is not worth pursuing the idea, and it would be safer to hire a nearby manège instead. That said, there should be no reason why you can't build a couple of portable cross-country fences; these are increasingly popular in cross-country courses, and it means you can move them to fresh ground, and reap the benefits that way.

CHAPTER 3

CONSTRUCTING EQUINE ENCLOSURES

Of all the large domesticated animals, horses and ponies are the most difficult to keep fenced in. They are powerful and intelligent creatures that seem to know, with unfailing regularity, exactly where the frail sections of a fence are. Normally, however, this behaviour is associated with poor management, in that only when their grazing has become so sparse do they feel driven to look elsewhere for a meal. Most horses will happily graze within a well-built enclosure if their owner/keeper maintains a high standard of care. Having said that, with horses there is always an unpredictable element, and the possibility of escape should always be taken into account when planning and building a barrier fence.

There is an impressive choice of fence style available on the equestrian market, and materials range from the traditional, low cost post and rail timber, to the highly expensive PVC post and rail. Wire products include a PVC-coated netting called Netlon, designed to be highly tensioned and less likely to trap hoofs, and standard agricultural stock materials such as sheep netting and single wire (single-strand wire usually placed above the netting); the latter are a less costly alternative, but are not really an effective barrier as compared to post and rail.

The choice of fencing material is ultimately up to the person who looks after the livestock. Replacing a whole field-boundary fence might turn out to be a costly exercise, depending on the products used; for instance, PVC post and rail, although designed to give long life, can work out at around £40 per metre (2004 prices), and for some, to enclose a 100m × 100m field with PVC is almost unjustifiably expensive. Nevertheless, PVC fencing excels in its ability to withstand the usual decay dilemmas associated with timber, and because it is uniquely designed for equestrian needs, typical maintenance difficulties are also catered for. The fencing rails, for instance, do not require nails, as they lock or snap into the pre-mortised posts, and if an animal were to push them off, they are easily pushed back into place. However, PVC has undesirable environmental effects attached to its use, and if you are after sustainable development, then it should be avoided.

To cope with today's demanding market and climatic conditions, orthodox fencing has come a long way. The problems relating to fungus and wood rot have been addressed with treatments that can extend the life of wood for many years, and because of this, timber still remains the most popular choice for boundary fencing.

A post slammer attached to a tractor's PTO makes for easy post erection.

Constructing a Post and Rail Fence

The first project describes the construction of a 328ft × 328ft (100m × 100m) post and rail fence, 4ft (1.2m) in height, using square posts and square rails, with four courses of horizontal rail as the stock-proof barrier, and incorporating a suitable access point for vehicles and horses. The scale of this project is only to give an idea of the relative calculations; those provided are suitable for the smaller equine, and measurements should be scaled up when constructing a paddock fence for a horse. When determining the area of land necessary to meet your particular circumstances you should seek the advice of someone well versed in equine husbandry; however, it is generally considered that at least an acre of land per horse will be required if it is to be kept at grass.

Tools and Materials

The following tools will be required:

- Spade (for excavating postholes)
- Crowbar (ideal for loosening compacted soil and breaking stone in a posthole)
- Hand saw (used for trimming posts and rails)
- Power drill, hand drill or rechargeable drill (used for pre-drilling rails before fixing them to the posts)

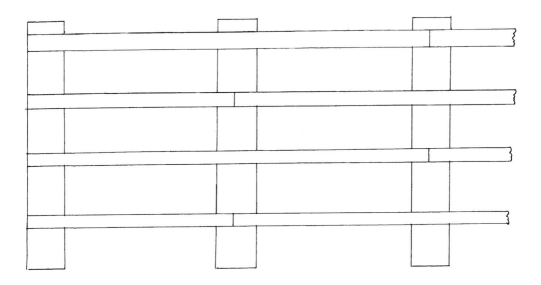

Post and rail fencing showing crossed joins.

- Claw hammer
- Spirit level or post leveller (used to align fencing posts. A post leveller is the ideal choice because it enables inspection of both sides at the same time, minimizing the risk of mistakes)
- Tape measure
- 100m of nylon string line (essential for correct post alignment)
- Fencing pliers and wire cutters (only needed if an old post and wire fence has to be taken apart)
- G-cramp or other clamping device (for holding a fencing rail against a post whilst nailing on)

The materials that would be required for a 100m × 100m enclosure are these:

- 222 × 6ft × 3in × 4in (1.6m × 7cm × 10cm) square, unpointed posts
- 444 × 12ft × 3.5in (3.6m × 7.2cm) square rails
- 1 × 8ft × 7in × 7in (2.4m × 17.5cm × 17.5cm) gate post (or stoop)
- 1 × 8ft × 6in × 6in (2.4m × 15cm × 15cm) gate clapper post
- 1 × 10ft (3m) field gate; this will be wide enough for vehicles as well
- A complete set of hook and band field-gate furniture, and an auto field-gate catch set; all these sets come complete with fixings
- 4/5in (10/13cm) galvanized nails
- Sand, gravel and cement (for settling in the gate posts)

Before You Start

Before the new fence can be built there are a few essential, and sometimes legal, procedures to consider. If the boundary fence borders a neighbour's garden or field you must ensure that it doesn't encroach onto their land: this means that the positioning of all the posts must be accurate. The deeds to your property should define where the boundaries lie, and who is responsible for maintaining them. Moreover, there is every possible chance that you may not be entitled to replace the section of fencing separating the two plots of land: if the existing boundary fence is still suitable for the purpose for which it was originally intended, even though it is not strong enough for a horse, then your neighbour will have no lawful obligation to change it; but the onus will still be on *you* to stop your animals escaping through it.

A simple negotiation with your neighbour might settle this problem. You can, for instance, establish another fence line, making sure it remains within your property even though you will lose a certain amount of grazing. If you are serious about the security of your animals, then the better option is to offer to replace the existing fence at your own cost, assuring your neighbour that the new one will be better and stronger than the original.

If a public right of way crosses your property there will be associated legal ramifications that you will have to consider. To start with, it is illegal to obstruct a public footpath or bridleway, and you should bear in mind a suitable access point when purchasing materials: thus, for a footpath you will be required to provide a wooden stile, and a gate for a bridleway, and they must be situated on the 'definitive line' as depicted on the local authority's 'Definitive Maps'. If you are not sure about these legal aspects, or the position of the path's definitive line, you should refer your case to the Footpaths Officer, who is normally attached to a local authority's Highways Department, and will be able to help you at no extra charge.

It may seem an easier option to reposition the access point, but this course of action is also highly illegal. To officially divert a public right of way is a complicated procedure that may not be worth the money you will have to spend, especially when most footpath diversion disputes invariably go in favour of the objectors who want to keep their footpath intact. To save you the extra expense of purchasing stile materials, you could position your own gateway on the definitive line so that the path or bridleway forms part of your own field access.

The following project tracks the construction of a new enclosure where one side forms a boundary owned by another landowner; an arrangement has been established to replace the neighbour's fence with new, horse-proof materials. It has also been ascertained that no public right of way bisects the land.

Dismantling the Existing Fence

The first phase of the work is to dismantle the existing fence, which begins by taking out the original stock-proof material. If the fence contains tensioned wire, in most cases strainer posts and struts will support it. Corner strainers will be braced by two of these struts; one will be holding the wire tension on the part you are about to dispose of, and the other will be set at 90 degrees, coping with the strain of the other wire. Be sure that you only dispose of the strut on the section of the fence that is going to be replaced: disturbing the second strut will result in loss of tension on the section of your neigh-

bour's fence that you wish to remain intact. One last point: do not disturb struts until both wire and netting have been taken down. Doing so will cause the strainer post to lean over.

For stock netting, use the gouge part of the fencing pliers to loosen staples. This is accomplished by placing the point of the gouge between the post and the staple, and then levering. If the staple is deeply embedded, tap the hammer end of the pliers with the claw hammer to force the gouge between the staple and the wood; this will pull the staple out. Then use the pincer end of the fencing pliers to extract it completely. Finally, store the staple in a safe container.

When removing fencing rails, use a lever bar or hammer to wrench them off the stakes. In older fences, where the nails have rusted, greater force may be required and in this case the greater leverage of a crowbar may come in useful. Once the rails have been extracted, bend the points of the nails to minimise risk of injury should anyone – man or beast – inadvertently stand on them.

Pulling old fencing stakes can sometimes be a frustrating and risky task, particularly if decay has set in below ground. This may not be evident until the force used to loosen them within their postholes actually causes them to break off, sending the fencer crashing to the ground, stake and all. Most posts, however, will pull out without any problems, and the technique used is simple. Grip the post with both hands somewhere near the top, and manoeuvre it backwards and forwards, and from side to side. Continue like this until it is loose enough to be lifted out.

If it still refuses to move, hammer in a 5in (13cm) nail about a foot from ground level, leaving just an inch or so proud of the wood. Tie a small length of strong rope around the post, just below the shank of the nail; attach the other end of the rope to a crowbar, leaving about 5in between it and the stake. Place the tip of the bar on the ground. Carefully taking hold of the opposite end, lever upward until the stake begins to move.

Posts that have been dug in, such as strainers, can be more difficult to budge, and the deeper in they are, the more suction there will be at the base of the hole; this is caused by moisture, and occurs frequently in areas with a high water table. Even seemingly loose posts can refuse to move, and the only way to deal with them is to dig with a spade or pull them out with a winch. To make life easier, there is no structural reason why these difficult posts shouldn't remain as part of the new fence if they are still in sound condition. Pulling out stakes will leave open postholes, which must be filled as a matter of course.

Digging in the Posts

The first step in fence construction is deciding where to start. In this case, since part of the neighbour's boundary has been stripped bare, it is only good manners to begin here and complete the whole of this section before building the rest of the fence. A linear fence is a strong fence, and the object of this assignment is to set the posts in a straight line from corner to corner. To achieve this effectively, select the most convenient end of the open boundary (usually the one near the materials store) to excavate the first posthole. It may be that a corner post on the neighbouring boundary is already in place. If this is the case, and at least 4ft

(1.2m) of it is standing proud, then you should use that as the starting point.

If there is no such existing post, then a new hole should be excavated to a depth of 2ft (60cm) and to twice the width of the post. Insert the post carefully into the hole, with the longer 4in (10cm) side facing into the field. Push two spadefuls of soil back into the hole, evenly surrounding the post's base. Next, tamp the soil down firmly with either the blunt end of a pointed fencing stake or a small piece of rail (you may be able to use the materials of the old fence for this). The post should now stand erect without any need of support. With a spirit level or post leveller, check the stake's alignment, and adjust as required. Use stone or old brick, if available, to help firm in the post, then push a further three or four spadefuls of soil back into the hole. Tamp down as before, keeping a check on the levels. Spade in another layer of matter and tamp down again, and continue like this until the hole has been refilled and the post is firm.

The next job is to insert the post at the far end of the area, working to the method just described.

With the two corners in position we now have an idea of the exact course this section will take. To achieve a straight line of stakes you will need to use the string line, stretched tightly from corner to corner; it should be set to run down the stock side of the enclosure (the side that will face the animal). Note that in windy conditions the string will blow around, making it difficult to align the posts, and to alleviate this problem two support posts should be dug in, positioned at equal intervals down the section.

Before digging in these two posts their precise position in the boundary must be worked out: it is important to appreciate that the uprights in a post and rail fence must be accurately placed, at 6ft (1.8m) intervals, to allow for the effective insertion of the rails. You can work out these distances by laying a complete course of rails between the two corners, making sure that each rail end is tightly butted up to the other. Each join will represent the position for a posthole, at every 12ft (3.6m) (the rails can stay on the ground as a guide to positioning the remaining posts); a 6ft template (a rail sawn to size) is then used as a guide for the stakes in between. Alternatively one could use a tape measure, but it may become monotonous considering the number of posts that require spacing.

Assuming that the string line is working correctly, the task of digging the rest of the posts can go ahead. Using the 6ft template, place it down on top of the first 12ft rail, making sure that both the 12ft and the 6ft rail ends are flush with the outside edge of the corner post. To ascertain the correct location for the next posthole, position the spirit level against the opposite end of the template. Hold the level vertical, and adjust it so that it is just touching the string, and the bubble is settled between the two level-markers. Place a marker on the ground and excavate another 2ft hole. Insert the next post, and use the spirit level to adjust it vertically to the string line. The post should just touch the string without pushing it out of line. Firm it up as described earlier. The remaining stakes should be inserted working to the same method, and making sure that the join between each two rails is centred on the post's face. If for some reason parts of the ground are difficult to dig, it is acceptable

to reposition a post, but always move it back down the line.

Fixing on the Rails

The next stage is to affix the four courses of rails. At this stage, no matter how firm the posts are, there is always the likelihood that hammering in nails could loosen a post in its hole, and the risk of this increases the higher up the post you go. A way to avoid this happening is to stand behind the upright, using your body as a brace. If the terrain is relatively even, then the rails can be attached and adjusted with a spirit level. But not many of us are that lucky, and the surface of our fields is often irregular, with humps and bumps of varying size and shape. Nevertheless, it is crucial that the equine fence remains at the optimum height, regardless of the lie of the land, and the best method to achieve this is to use a template to assist in positioning the rails. The template should be no more than 4ft, with even spacer-marks for the four courses.

When connecting rails it is essential that each course begins where the first post was inserted. This is vital if some of these posts were repositioned due to ground difficulties. Start by lifting the first rail and clamping it to the second post (the one that is 6ft from the corner), and aligning it with the 4ft template mark. Next, tack the rail to the post by driving a nail half-way in. Go to the corner stake and pre-drill two holes, one near the top, the other close to the bottom edge, ensuring they are at least 1in from the rail end. Align the rail end with the template, and drive in two nails. The clamp can now be released from the second upright. Check the far rail-end against the template, pre-drill it, and fix it to the post.

The second level of rail should be connected below, only this time it will be 6ft in length. The reason for this is that the joins on each course of rail must be crossed or bridged, because this adds further strength to the enclosure. There is no written rule that states the distances between courses, but for appearance' sake, the spaces between each course should appear equal. To work out these distances, measure the area from the bottom edge of the top rail to the ground, and divide by three. Knowing the total height of the fence is 4ft, minus 3in (7.6cm) for the width of the top rail, we are left with 45in (1.14m). Dividing forty-five by three comes to a final total of 15in (38cm). Transpose this measurement to the template.

After pre-drilling and attaching the 6ft rail, connect a third, 12ft timber to the course below. The bottom course will be another 6ft length. By affixing 12ft rails to the remainder of this section of fence the joins will be bridged by default. To complete the enclosure, follow the methods just described.

The Universal Stock Fence

Many people, especially smallholders, keep two or more species of animal, and sometimes grazing land is managed with a mix of species browsing the same paddock. Or it is possible that your neighbour keeps sheep and you have ponies, a situation that may generate a conflict of approach when it comes to containing both safely: what is fine for a cow is dangerous for a small pony, and your goat could be off down the road visiting friends and posing a traffic hazard. Needless to say, with a mix of livestock you will almost certainly have to come to a compromise regarding fencing style, if you are not to compromise security.

One solution is to take the three most popular types of fence and roll them into one entity: this would solve the problem for most, if not all the grazing animals a smallholder is likely to keep. Stock netting for sheep, rails for goats and ponies, and strong posts for the cow with an itchy rump, can all be pieced together to form an effective, long-lasting enclosure requiring little maintenance. Structurally, however, all stock fences have one element in common: the stock-proof material, whether rail or wire, is secured to the 'stock side' (the part of the fence facing the animal), thus ensuring that the nails holding the wood and the staples fastening the netting stay in place if livestock pushes or rubs up against it.

Materials and Tools

For most people, one of the main concerns against constructing a new fence is the cost of the materials; but continually having to repair an unsuitable or weak fence could, in the long run, turn out to be more expensive than purchasing new items that will last for years. The following is a list of the materials needed to build a 164ft × 164ft (50m × 50m) mixed stock enclosure, and the best fencing tools and stock netting to use:

- Fencing stakes: 111 × 5ft × 3in (1.5m × 7cm) round, pointed stakes. This equates to one stake every 6ft (1.8m)

- Fencing rails: 167 × 12ft × 3in (3.6m × 7.62cm) half-round rails. This will be enough to attach a course of three rails around the new enclosure
- Stock netting: 4 × 164ft (50m) rolls of medium-tensile stock netting
- Nails: 5kg (11lb) 4in or 5in (10cm or 12cm) galvanized nails
- Fencing staples: 5kg (11lb) galvanized

You will also need the following tools:

- Post slammer or fencing maul (used for knocking in fencing stakes. A fencing maul looks like a sledgehammer, but is made of brittle cast iron. It is only intended for hitting wood, and if you use it for breaking stone or driving metal pins you will shatter the end. A maul requires accuracy when post knocking otherwise it could split the top of the stake and injure the fencer. A post slammer is a steel tube with a closed end and a handle on each side. It is placed over the top of the stake and used to drive the stake into the ground. With this method there is less risk of an accident, as such it is the preferred option for most fencing jobs. For health and safety reasons a safety helmet should be worn with any tool that is raised above head height)
- Crowbar (essential for starting post-holes)
- Claw hammer (for driving home staples and nails)
- Fencing pliers (an inexpensive, universal fencing tool, complete with a grip for wire tensioning, wire cutters, small hammer, a gouge for releasing difficult fencing staples, a staple puller and a 'turner' for bending wire ends)

Health and Safety Precautions

- Leather safety gloves
- Steel toe-capped boots or wellingtons
- Waterproof clothing
- Safety helmet
- First-aid kit

- Bar strainer (this tool has a long bar and hinged foot/wire-grip, and is ideal for tensioning small lengths of netting of around 10m)
- Chain strainer (by far the best implement for straining wire and netting. Capable of applying the strongest force to heavy-duty netting)
- String line (for ensuring accurate post alignment)
- Spirit level
- Tape measure

Setting Out the Posts

As soon as the correct boundary lines have been established, the task of building the fence can begin. Start by inserting the four corner posts: this will provide the basic shape of the enclosure. To ensure the accurate alignment of intermediate posts, a string line should be tied from one corner to the other. The string should be attached on the stock side, half-way up the stakes, and pulled tightly.

Working on the 'non stock side', the intermediate stakes can now be knocked into the ground. Unlike a post and wire fence, where accurate spacing between the intermediates is not an important structural consideration, this fence style requires a considerable amount of precision. If the gap between the stakes is too long, you will not be able to fasten the ends of the rails to the posts: the importance of this structural factor cannot be emphasized enough.

The easy way to make sure that the rails will fit the posts is to use one of the fencing rails as a template. First, the 6ft or half-way point should be clearly marked on the rail, then it should be placed on the ground, ensuring that the rail end comes flush with the outside of the corner post. Adjust the rail so that it is aligned with the string line on the stock side of the fence. With a crowbar, place a pointer on the ground next to the 6ft template mark, and do the same at the rail end furthest from the corner. The crowbar, in effect, represents the centre of a post, and if you work to the method just described the fencing rails should fit the posts accurately.

Knocking in the Posts

With the ground plainly marked, remove the template and hold the crowbar vertically to the string line. Remembering that the crowbar represents the centre of the posts, move it back 1.5in from the string to its final position. Ram the bar into the ground, then pull it back no more than 40 degrees: in this position, turn it 360 degrees round the hole for a few times. Lift the bar out and repeat the procedure again, pushing deeper into the posthole whilst making sure it remains vertical. Carry on like this until the posthole is at least 6–7in deep. Take a fencing post and literally ram it into the posthole; it shouldn't need any support. Using a spirit level, adjust the stake until it is vertical and just touching the string. From this point onward it is a matter of knocking the stake home. Drive the post

down at least 1.5ft, adjusting it with the spirit level as necessary.

The second posthole should be started in exactly the same way, but before driving the stake home use the 12ft rail to check for exact spacing. The end of the rail should just reach the centre of the new post, allowing ample room to attach the next rail. Repeat this procedure for the rest of the stakes.

Bracing the Posts

The next phase deals with the wire netting, but before it can be stapled on, the posts will need bracing. A standard post and wire fence uses hefty strainer posts and struts to stop the corner posts from leaning with the tension of the wire, but the method used for this project exploits the horizontal, rigid properties of the top rails. Starting from one corner, secure a complete course of top rails around the enclosure's perimeter. In hilly areas it is normal practice to follow the shape of the ground in order to achieve an even gap between top and bottom. A wooden baton with a guide mark can aid you with this. A height of around 3.5ft (1m) is suitable for most animals, and if workable, leave around 2in of post above the rail. This is really for the aesthetic value of the job, rather than structural significance, as it allows for even post topping. Remember to pre-drill the rails, otherwise they can split, and use two 4in or 5in nails at each point.

Stapling on the Wire

A roll of stock netting is made up of two horizontal, high-tensile straining wires, one at the top and the other on the bottom. These wires should be tensioned with heavy-duty straining tools such as chain strainers. The remaining horizontal wires are low tensile, and should only be pulled using lightweight tools such as a pair of fencing pliers.

On a corner post, staple all the horizontal strands to the wood using two staples 1in (2.5cm) apart on each wire, making sure to leave at least 1in of wire end free. Drive the staples in as far as they will go. Bend the wire ends down about 45 degrees, and hammer in another staple over each one.

Next, roll the netting for 25m up the line of stakes and stand it upright, making sure the wire is touching each post. If the roll falls down, push the crowbar through the centre. Tension the top high-tensile wire, and secure it with three staples driven home, only this time the wire strand should remain horizontal. Repeat this for the bottom wire. The intermediate, low-tensile wires can now be pulled using the fencing pliers, and stapled on. Go back down the line and secure the netting to the rest of the stakes. This time, however, leave a slight air gap between wire and fixing to allow for natural expansion and contraction of the galvanized metal.

Roll the netting to the next corner, tension it, and staple it on. Cut the wire, leaving at least 1in of free wire end to bend over and staple. Repeat these procedures to attach the remaining netting.

Fixing the Lower Rails

Affixing the lower and middle courses of rail is more or less the same as the top course, the only difference being that the joins should be crossed. To achieve this, begin the middle course with a 6ft length, and continue the course with twelve-footers. On the lower part use twelve-footers again.

A Combination Fence

Some fencers put the rails on the stock side and the netting on the non-stock side, but there is a risk a goat or a horse could trap its hoof between the two. Even with the project described above, horned goats could push their heads through the wire, leaving them trapped. Netting isn't really suitable for equines as they can paw at the wire, which could lead to a trapped hoof; but this can be avoided to a degree if the netting is tensioned.

This is a combination fence designed for smallholders with limited room; however, if enough space is available to accommodate the animals separately, then the correct enclosures for each species should be built.

Particular Problems

Fencing on Hills

The method for hill fencing only differs slightly from fencing on the flat, so refer to the techniques described at the beginning of this chapter. The important differences are essential, and should be followed closely; they are as follows:

- Ensure that the posts are vertical at all times, and do not lean with the slope.
- If the boundary runs parallel to the foot of the hill, build this particular section on flatter ground, and at least one stride from the foot of the slope if at all possible. Equines can jump and use hills near fences as a springboard.

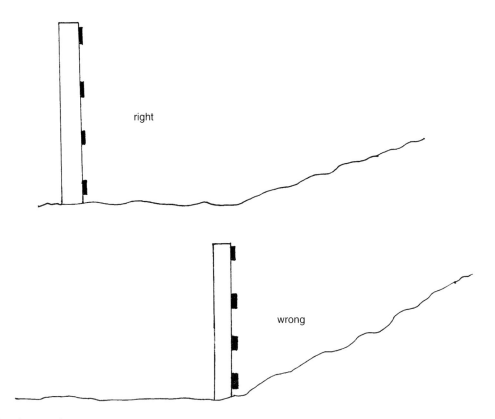

Fencing on slopes.

A secondary, less effective solution is to raise the height of the fence. The danger with this method is that the boundary will become top heavy.

Fencing for the Destructive Horse

Equine stock can show little respect for fencing if they have a mind to escape. The weak points of a fencing rail are around the wood knots, and this is an unavoidable fault as most rails are made of pine. For small ponies the problem can be solved by using sturdy, 12ft × 3.5in half-round rails, but instead of securing them against the side of the posts, rest them on the very top with the rounded side facing up. Larger ponies and horses will require a different solution, especially if they are master escapees. One solution is to raise the enclosure to the height of the animal's neck, but that would mean purchasing stronger and larger posts and could result in an unsightly, top-heavy fence if built incorrectly. Some people suggest using barbed wire; however, personally I think this is a dangerous alternative and one that should never be used near horses.

During my experience as a landscape contractor I have dealt with this problem using two methods. The first is a cost-effective measure involving the use of two lengths of tensioned single wire (single-strand wire normally used as top wire for stock fences) attached to the top of the rails. Although this won't stop the rails from breaking, it will keep the top of the fence together, extending the life of the enclosure.

The second method is slightly more expensive as it requires the use of an electric fence. Electric fences have come a long way in recent times and you can now pick up a small battery unit that will secure an average-sized enclosure. Near the top of every fence post attach a wooden baton or metal bracket of between 6–8in (15–20cm) in length, preferably at an upward, 45-degree angle. Next, secure

the electric fence wire to the ends of the baton with the fencing staples driven in half way so that the electric wire will have easy travel. Most importantly, place the electric wire on your side of the fence. As a reminder to yourself and others, make use of electric fence warning signs at regular intervals down the length of the paddock. This fence should act as an effective deterrent to any horse putting undue pressure on the rails.

Further information about the various methods employed in stock fencing, including ideas to solve common problems and the installation of wooden stiles and gates, can be found in my book *A Guide to Stock Fencing* (The Crowood Press, 2002).

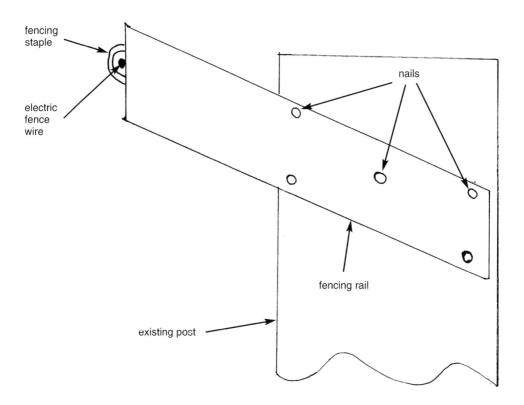

fencing staple

electric fence wire

nails

fencing rail

existing post

Affixing an electric fence barrier to an existing enclosure.

CHAPTER 4

A BRIEF GUIDE TO PLANNING PERMISSION

The information in this chapter is to serve merely as a guide, and you should always seek advice and guidance from your local planning authority or planning expert. Each of Britain's local councils works to the rules laid down in the Town and Country Planning Act 1990; however, there is a plethora of other legislation governing land-use planning. The latter's role is to set the framework for the development and use of land, taking full account of economic, social and environmental issues. Land-use planning oversees the construction of new development on private, agricultural and industrial landscapes, and helps to ensure that all new development is in keeping with the local landscape and an area's 'local plan' – or more recently, its 'unitary development plan'.

Planning permission, and if or when it is required, is possibly the most confusing subject relating to equine ownership. In some cases it is required for keeping horses, and for any building to accommodate them: the keeping of horses and provision of livery facilities is not regarded as agricultural use, and changing the use of land from farming to equine activities may require planning consent. But many families own horses for their own personal use, and for the most part, planning con-

sent would not be required where it is small scale.

Keeping equines at a private house would not usually require planning permission, but there are other regulations that may impact on your plans. For example, if you plan to keep your animal in a small, town-style garden as opposed to a field of around one acre, you may soon find yourself visited by the local Environmental Health Department should your neighbours make a complaint of nuisance – quite apart from animal welfare considerations. You may be required to apply for a 'change of use' directive if, for example, your garden or land is presently used for something else.

Where a permanent construction is concerned, you must assume that you need to apply for permission to build it. Mobile field shelters do not require planning permission, but if the field you keep your horses on requires it for change of use, then the shelter may also be controlled by the consent. Some types of structure do require planning consent, including permanent field shelters and stables if they are above a certain size. Other equestrian structures such as indoor arenas and manèges will require a planning authorization, as do some cross-country jumps. Temporary jumps do not require planning permission.

The Planning Process

As previously mentioned, the planning process can be very confusing, and before submitting a planning application it is a good idea to pay your local planning office a visit to take a look at previous, similar applications. You are entitled to do this because all current applications are available for the public to look at and comment on. If you want to see other, older applications then you may have to pay a small fee for the privilege, but the journey could yield important information about the way to submit your own application, and the decision you could expect. Whilst you are there you could check whether or not your proposed development actually requires planning permission. Developers are encouraged to talk to planning officers prior to the submission of an application. It may be better, in the long term, to consult an independent expert and subsequently engage them to act on your behalf if necessary. This would be particularly important if your plans are large scale, in a sensitive area – for example, a national park – or close to residential areas.

To begin the planning process, first contact your local council, stating what the development proposal will be. In return they should forward to you the relevant documents to complete, along with information as to how much it will cost you (this varies depending on the local authority). You may be asked to provide an architect's drawing if the proposals involve a new building, or the conversion of an existing building. The format of the drawing can vary from council to council,

and if the planning authority has not supplied this information, you must ask for the details. An experienced architect would know the authority's usual requirements. Some suppliers of prefabricated stables, or manège builders, will supply drawings for planning use, or even engage in the process on your behalf. You will also need a site plan, to show the exact location of the development proposals, and the land within which the applicant has an interest; this can generally be purchased from the local planning authority.

It is a statutory requirement that a council attempts to determine an application within eight weeks. Within this period your immediate neighbours (called 'adjoining occupiers') will be notified of the proposal. Your neighbours will receive a letter from the council, describing the development and allowing them the opportunity to comment on it: this is their right. Their comments will be recorded on the planning system, and placed in the same file as your application. Local councillors will also be notified of the application, and a notice will be placed on a suitable point on the public highway, near to the point of the development, to allow members of the public an opportunity to comment on the proposals.

The application may be determined by delegated powers; in this case an officer will decide the outcome. This will only happen for minor applications, where there are no objections. Generally, applications are determined at a planning meeting attended by the elected councillors of the area. The planning officer will draft out a report on your application, giving a brief outline of the proposals and any relevant planning guidance, and a record of any objections received. The report's conclusion will be a recommendation for granting or refusing the application, along with the reasons for the recommendation. The elected members will decide the application.

There may or may not be any discussion, depending on the circumstances; generally councillors accept their officer's recommendation unless they are lobbied by the local population. Some local authorities will allow people to speak at their planning meetings; if you want to do this you should contact the committee clerk beforehand. The officer's recommendation should be available a few days before the committee meeting.

If your application is granted, there will usually be conditions attached. These may specify the timescale within which the development has to be completed, or they may prevent certain activities taking place. They are generally used to protect the amenity of the locality. If an application is refused, it would be because it didn't comply with planning guidance or the law. Either way you will be informed in writing of the council's decisions, and the reasons for their ruling.

If planning permission is refused, and/or the conditions imposed are considered unreasonable, you have the right of appeal. However, anyone considering this course of action should seek expert representation, as the legal costs can be extremely high should the appeal fail.

This type of structure will almost certainly require planning permission.

CHAPTER 5

BUILDING A MOBILE LOOSEBOX

The advantage of a mobile loosebox (a stable that can be moved around the paddock) is that it doesn't require planning permission, and obviously it can be moved around to suit the weather and ground conditions. To stay on the right side of planning law, however, the structure will have to be moved on a regular basis so that it doesn't become 'permanent'.

Before committing yourself to this venture there are two essential facts to consider. First, the terrain on which the structure is to be sited should be free from major obstacles and relatively flat. Another important necessity is an appropriate vehicle to move it with: at the least it will need to be strong, and four-wheel drive, preferably with a low-ratio gear option for extra traction in the wet; but even this isn't ideal, and the recommended towing vehicle is a tractor.

Design and Materials

The following project describes the construction of a simple, 10ft × 8ft (3m × 2.4m) loosebox, suitable for just one small pony. All the required materials can be purchased from the outlets already described in this book, with the possible

exception of the drawbar (the towing mechanism) and the steel chassis to which it has to be bolted (explained later). Some concessions have been made so as to keep the weight down, the most obvious being the lack of a constructed floor.

It is easier to build the loosebox if the wall panels are prefabricated in a workshop on a large workbench, or failing that, on a large flat concrete area close to the paddock site. They should be actually assembled in the paddock to avoid any difficulties of access. The mobile stable for this project consists of four wall panels, all 8ft high, with two 10ft long and the other two 8ft long; one of the 10ft panels will have the door-frame. The drawbar and towing section will be bolted to the underside of the loosebox. To keep the method of construction simple, the roof will be flat, sloping towards the back; this style of roof can be just as effective as the 'apex' variety, and is certainly easier to build. Guttering is an optional feature.

Choosing suitable roofing materials is important with regard to the building's lifespan. There is a vast choice of substances on the market, and they will all do an adequate job, but some are better than others. The popular styles include roofing felt secured to timber panels or boards, corrugated galvanized sheeting, and corrugated plastic sheeting – and each of these has advantages and disadvantages. Felt, for instance, is simple to work with, it can be trimmed to size quickly, and it looks aesthetically pleasing if laid properly; on the down side, it tears quite easily, making it susceptible to wind damage. Galvanized sheeting has an endless lifespan, it won't rip, and it rarely becomes dislodged in windy conditions; on the other hand it is heavy and clumsy, very difficult to cut, and it looks unsightly. Corrugated plastic is lightweight, and little effort is needed when applying it to a roof; but it can eventually become brittle.

The best material on the market is called 'Onduline', a strong, lightweight corrugated roofing material. Developed around fifty years ago, and manufactured from bitumen-saturated organic fibres, it is fast becoming the first choice for agricultural, industrial and domestic use. To all intents and purposes Onduline resembles a plastic, and as such it is easy to cut with a saw and can be fixed to timbers with a hammer. It is not susceptible to weathering, nor will it become brittle as time wears on. This material can be purchased from most DIY outlets.

The following materials will be required:

- 30 × 12ft × 3in × 2in (3.6m × 7.6cm × 5cm) timber rails (for constructing the frame studs)
- 68 × 10ft × 6in (3m × 15cm) tongue-and-groove boarding (sometimes called sidings). Tongue-and-groove can be purchased in a variety of thicknesses: 0.5, 0.75 to 1in (1.2cm, 1.9cm to 2.5cm). As this is an external structure and likely to sustain an element of stress, it

may be advisable to choose one of the 0.75 or 1in options
- 2 × 12ft × 6in × 2in (3.6m × 15cm × 5cm) timber boards (for the box's skids)
- 7 × 12ft × 4in × 2in (3.6m × 10cm × 5cm) rails (for the roofing joists)
- 2 × 8ft × 3in × 2in (2.4m × 7.6cm × 5cm) timber rails (for connecting the skids together)
- 1 × 10ft × 6in × 1in timber board (as an 'eaves' at the front of the building)
- 8 × 8ft × 4ft × 1in (2.4m × 1.2m × 2.5cm) oriented strand board (OSB), for kick boarding
- 8ft (1.2m) of threaded rod, complete with 12 washers and nuts
- 5kg of 5in (127mm) galvanized nails
- 5kg of 2in (50mm) galvanized 'splitless' nails. These fixings are designed for tongue-and-groove. They come with thin shanks and blunt points, which helps to reduce the risk of wood splitting. For best results and greater adhesion, nails with ring-threaded or spiral-threaded shanks can be used
- 5kg of 3in (70mm) galvanized nails (for connecting horizontal studs)
- 4kg of Onduline nails
- 36 × 6in coach screws (for attaching the loosebox to the chassis)
- 8 galvanized steel plates with pre-drilled 10mm holes (for attaching the loosebox to the chassis)
- 32 × 10mm nuts and bolts, or four lengths of 10mm threaded rod (for attaching the loosebox to the chassis)

For the stable door materials, *see* chapter 8.

You will need the following tools:

- Hand saw or electric saw
- Power drill or rechargeable drill
- Claw hammer

- Tape measure
- Socket set or spanners
- 3 G-cramps or other clamping devices
- Pencil
- Set square

Important Safety Point

Building this structure in strong wind conditions is not recommended. For ease of construction, at least four able helpers should be enlisted, especially when assembling the wall panels.

Constructing the Loosebox

The 8ft Wall Panels

To begin, take two 12ft (3.6m) rails, and measure and saw them into 8ft (2.4m) lengths; mark one as 'top' and the other 'bottom'. Next, measure and saw a further five rails, this time into lengths of 92in (2.3m); this particular measurement is critical.

The next stage is to create a rectangle using four rails. Working with the 8ft rails, pre-drill two holes, through the 3in face, on each of the rail ends. Take two

Constructing the loosebox panels in a workshop.

92in timbers, and place one at each end of the 8ft rail at right angles. Making sure that all the rails are standing on their 2in surface areas and that each corner is flush, drive two 5in nails through each pre-drilled nail hole. Repeat this for the second 8ft timber. If you have not got the luxury of a workbench you may find it easier to brace the frame against a wall or similar immovable surface whilst hammering. To ensure that the measurements of the rectangle frame are correct, measure diagonally from the top left corner to the bottom right-hand corner, then measure from top right to bottom left. If both measurements work out the same, the frame is 'true'.

Installing the Studs

The next stage is to install the frame's intermediate timbers (called studs) using the remaining 92in rails. These must be inserted at 2ft (60cm) intervals inside the wall panel. The way to do this is to run a tape measure down the lengths of both top and bottom rails, marking every 2ft point with a set square and pencil. When measured, insert the first stud inside the frame and align it with the top and bottom 2ft marks. For accuracy, the pencil marks should be in line with the centres of the 92in rail ends. Before nailing on, inspect the distance between the first rail (the 92in timber at the end of the frame): the measurement should be equal, and the two timbers parallel. If the rail is bowed, which can be quite common, do not force it, as this will pose undue stress to the finished wall panel; it is much safer to leave it alone.

To complete the frame, connect the remaining 92in studs in exactly the same fashion. To give the frame some lateral stability, a row of horizontal studs, individually sawn to 22in (55cm), must be slotted between the vertical rails. These are usually placed at the vertical halfway point (4ft/1.2m). The horizontal studs can be affixed using 3in nails driven through at an angle.

The 10ft Wall Panels

The rear wall panel of the loosebox is fabricated in the same way as the 8ft panels. Obvious differences are in the lengths of the frame's horizontal timbers, which should be sawn down to 10ft as opposed to 8ft.

The front wall panel incorporates the door-frame, so the method of construction is slightly different. Build the initial rectangle as previously described, remembering to use 10ft horizontals as opposed to 8ft. Unlike the first panel, where the vertical studs were first inserted 2ft from one end, the priority here is to concentrate on the door-frame. The width of the stable doors will be 43in (1.08m), with the door-frame set into the centre of the panel. The proportions of the door-frame are critical, as it should allow for easy access, and should take into account future expansion and contraction of the wood; therefore the width between the door-frame uprights should be no less than 44in (1.1m). In this project the total height of the two doors is 7ft (84in = 2.1m), meaning that the vertical opening area will be no less than 85in. The construction of the stable doors is discussed later.

Making the Door-Frame

To measure up for the door-frame, take a measurement of 38in (96cm) from the

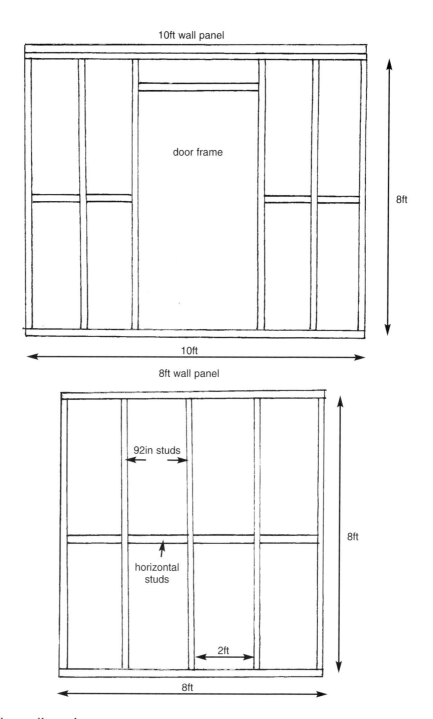

Mobile loosebox wall panels.

bottom outside corner of the wall panel, and mark it on the bottom rail with a pencil. Repeat this measurement from the top outside corner, marking the top rail, and then do the same from the other side. The measurements between the marks, on the top and bottom timbers, should be 44in. Next insert one 92in rail, aligning it with the top and bottom marks, and secure it with 5in nails, two driven in through the bottom timber and two through the top. Connect the second 92in rail against the second set of marks. The door-frame uprights are now in position.

The next sets of measurements are for the top of the door-frame. Working from the wall-panel's bottom rail, measure 85in towards the top and place a mark on the door-frame timber. Do the same for the opposite timber. Next, take another 12ft rail, measure 44in, mark it, and cut it with a hand saw. Carefully aligning the bottom face of the off-cut with the 85in marks, connect it to the frame using 5in nails, two from either side.

The need to keep the loosebox light in weight has meant that the space within is limited, and every available option to maintain this space must be taken. For reasons of health and safety all stable doors should open outwards, rather than inwards, and the doorstop, a length of baton 1in × 1in nailed to the vertical length of the frame, ought to be positioned to accommodate this. Here the doorstop is connected to the 3in face and adjacent to the back edge of the upright. The door-frame is now complete.

For the remaining studs, measure from each side of the panel to the door-frame, and halve the totals. The gaps will not be 2ft, but that doesn't matter.

Joining the Frames Together

The four frames are assembled using two fixing methods. First, they are bolted to one another on each of the corners, top and bottom. Further nuts, bolts and washers are then used half-way down the frame's uprights. Then to make it even more secure, nails or screws are driven through. Joining the frames is a job for more than one person, and it is best achieved on a flat surface.

The first step is to pre-drill all the uprights. The size of drill bit will depend on the diameter of the fixing used, but do not use anything less than 10mm. Working on both 10ft frames, measure around 2in from all the inside corners, and mark it on the 92in timbers with a pencil, then drill through to the other side, holding the tool level at all times.

The next stage is best performed with the frame vertical, and this is where the extra help would come in useful. With one 10ft section held upright, bring one of the 8ft frames to meet it at a right angle, ensuring that its 3in face meets the 2in edge of the 10ft's upright. Before going any further, clamp them tightly with three G-cramps, one near each corner and the third near the middle, making sure that the outside corner is flush. The two sections can now stand unaided. To bore the holes for the 8ft frame, just drill through the holes already created.

Concentrate now on the threaded rod. With the hacksaw, cut three 7in lengths, guiding the blade as straight as possible. Take three nuts (one for each piece of rod) and twist them down at least 1in, then drop three washers over the opposite ends. Next, push the rods through the drill holes until the nuts and washers are set firmly against the timber. Place three more nuts and washers on the bare ends of the rods, and hand-tighten them to the frame. Lock them down using a socket and ratchet or a spanner, and then remove the clamps. Repeat this procedure for the remaining frames.

Attaching the Skids and Building the Chassis

The skid section is an individual construction in its own right. It has to be strong enough to sustain the entire structure's weight whilst being pulled

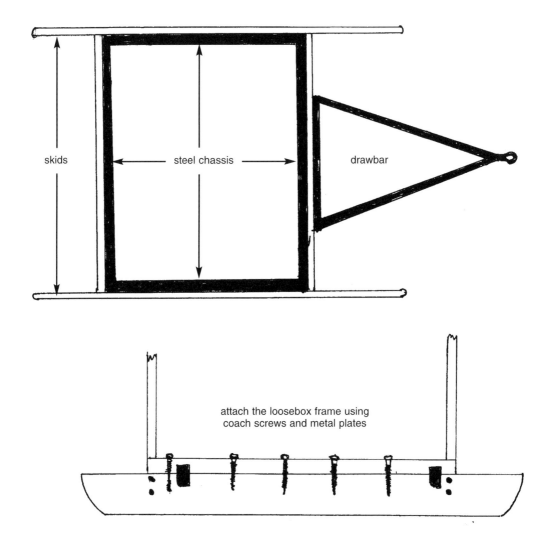

Mobile loosebox skid frame and chassis.

The drawbar of a mobile loosebox. Note the galvanized metal behind: added to the top of a stable door, this deters crib biting.

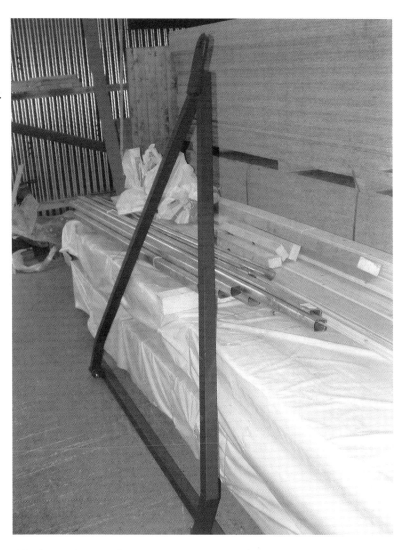

around a field or paddock, and it is for this reason that a professional welder, someone who is familiar with fashioning steel to suit any situation, should be employed. Even I would seek this assistance. For the most part, however, the basic shell of the chassis can be constructed before professional help is sought.

The only sawing that is needed is to shape the skids. The square ends of the 12ft × 6in × 2in boards should be angled and rounded off from the bottom to allow easier overland travel. The smaller, 8ft × 3in × 2in cross-members are bolted to the skids with the aid of galvanized steel brackets. The top edges of the 8ft boards must be level with the top edges of the skids, as a ground clearance of 3in must be maintained at all times. The cross-members should be 10ft apart to represent the length of the loosebox.

Now is the time to seek professional help. Ask the contractor to craft an internal steel chassis to fit inside the entire skid frame. The chassis is then bolted to the skids and the 8ft timbers. If a suitable drawbar hasn't been found, the contractor should be able to make one to your specifications. The towing mechanism, like the timbers, has to be bolted to the steel chassis.

The shell of the loosebox can now be lifted onto the chassis and fastened down using 4in coach screws through the bottom, horizontal rails. This will equate to two screws between each stud. Use galvanized steel plates with nuts and bolts to create 'strong points' near the four inside corners; the plates, of course, will connect the building to the chassis.

Constructing the Roof

The Roofing Timbers

As mentioned at the beginning of this chapter, the roof of the loosebox in this project slopes towards the back. Before the roof bearers (or joists) can be attached, the front 10ft wall panel will require a slight modification. Take another 12ft × 3in × 2in rail, saw it down to 10ft, and nail the 3in face to the top front, horizontal timber of the panel. This will create a 2in drop from front to back, the minimum slope one should create.

Now we are going to determine the exact position for each joist on the loosebox. With the tape measure, measure 20in (50cm) from one of the top outside corners. It doesn't matter which corner you start from, but be sure that the marks are drawn on the 10ft panels, and not the 8ft. From the first 20in mark,

measure the same distance again, and scribe a further marker; continue like this until you reach the end of the panel. Do the same for the top of the opposite 10ft panel. These marks now represent the centres of the roofing joists.

Place the first joist on its 2in edge, and bridge the gap between the two 10ft frames; then adjust the joist flush with the front of the 8ft panel. You will notice that the timber has not yet been sawn, and this is why. Alter the joist so that it overlaps both the front and back 10ft sections, and then, making sure it is still flush with the face of the 8ft, G-cramp it to the loosebox structure. Using a long straight-edge (a spirit level is ideal), place it against the corner of the building and the 4in side of the joist, then scribe a vertical line on the joist. Repeat this on the opposite end. Unclamp the joist and place it on a firm cutting surface, then carefully saw down the lines. The end of the joist, although at an angle, is now vertical with the box. Use this joist as a template for trimming down the remaining six timbers.

Working from one end, place the first joist on the frame, ensuring that it is true with both 8ft and 10ft wall panels. Drive in two 4in nails, at an angle, on either side of the timber; at least 2in of the shank must penetrate into the rail below. Repeat for the other end. To further secure the joist, a 6in nail or screw is driven in vertically from the top (to do this the holes must be pre-drilled). Place the second joist on the frame, fine tuning it to line up with the measurement marks on both sides. Fix it to the box as just described. Attach the remaining timbers using the same technique.

Looking at the front of the building, there are noticeable gaps between the bottom of the roofing timbers and the

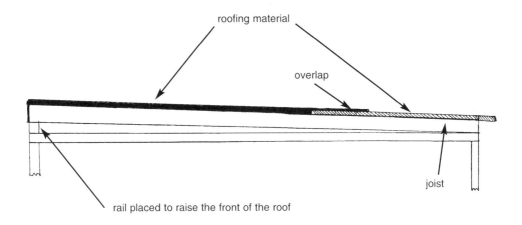

Roofing for the mobile loosebox.

frame. Although this appears unsightly, structurally the building is sound. Eventually, however, these joins will be hidden by the eaves.

Attaching the Roofing Sheets

The Onduline roofing system is designed to be attached in an 'overlap' fashion, to promote weatherproofing. Thus the lower portion of the roof should be covered first to allow the higher sheets to overlap, ensuring that rainwater will run off the whole roof, as opposed to through the first join, which is what would happen if the bottom materials were to cross over the top. To guarantee complete coverage, two of the roofing sheets will need to be sawn in half, a task best performed with a jig-saw; these sawn sheets can then be placed along the back section of roof.

Before nailing them on, it is advisable to do a dummy run first. If you are not fixing guttering, the sheeting should overlap the back of the box by at least 5in, ensuring that continual water run-off will not impact on the timber. Start from one end by laying the first sheet so that it overlaps the gable end by at least 2in. Lay the second sheet, with the same overlap, on the opposite gable. Now place the middle sheets, overlaying as much of the neighbouring panels as possible. Secure the panels to the joists below with the Onduline nails; you can drive them straight through the material. To complete the job, connect the remaining four, full-sized panels following the technique just described, making sure that the ends of the sheets are flush with the front of the loosebox.

Constructing the Outer Shell

With the frame complete, the next job is to install the outer shell of tongue-and-groove. Take sixteen lengths of siding, and measure and saw them down to 8ft. It is advisable to use an electric saw to minimize the risk of splitting, but careful use of a hand saw can achieve the same. There is only one way you can lay tongue-

Fixing tongue-and-groove boards.

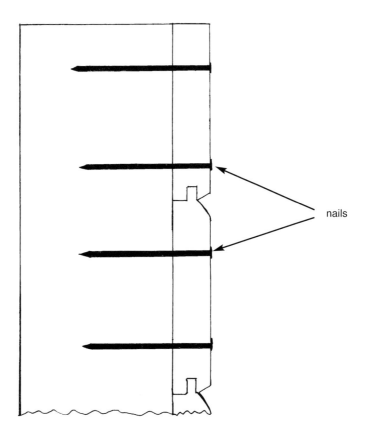

nails

and-groove when attaching it to buildings, and that is from the bottom of the frame with the 'tongue' facing towards the top. Place the first board, making sure it completely covers the timbers at both ends and on the bottom of the frame. Drive two nails through the board and into each stud, no less than 2in (5cm) apart. It is essential that the nails are affixed one above the other. Pre-drill at each end of the board to avoid splitting.

Take a second board, and slot the 'groove' into the 'tongue' of the first. Secure it to the studs using the same nailing method. It is bad practice to drive nails into the boards' interlocking sections, thereby physically joining them together: each board should be connected

individually, and the reason for this is movement. When timber is subjected to the elements it expands and contracts, and joining the boards to one another will very likely cause them to split. Finish this phase by covering the rest of the panels in the same fashion.

Affixing the Kick Boards

Kick boarding is attached to the internal wall studs and acts as a first-line defence against outer wall panel damage if the animal were to kick against it. The material used in commercially available units is usually oriented strand board (OSB), as it provides adequate strength with

Affixing the internal kick-boarding.

optimum workability. Kick boarding should be nailed to the studs – cutting it to size where necessary – and should cover the whole of the lower half of the loosebox up to a minimum height of 4ft (1.2m). If you prefer, OSB can be used as a wall-to-wall lining to act as insulation to some degree.

Putting Up the Eaves

It is now time to give the loosebox its finishing touch. Two lengths of tongue-and-groove boarding can be put up to serve as eaves on the sides of the building. To create the best possible bond as regards waterproofing, raise the boards slightly above the panels' horizontal timbers. The front eave (the 10ft × 6in × 1in board) should be positioned at the same level as the highest points of the roofing material. As additional waterproofing, a narrow length of impermeable membrane can be affixed to bridge the gap between the Onduline and the eave. Butyl is the best material, as it is resistant to ultra-violet light decay.

Building a Static Loosebox

The construction method for the mobile loosebox can be altered quite easily to

Mobile loosebox with apex roof.

A static loosebox and attached out-building with Onduline roofing. This particular building may require planning permission.

suit a static structure that sits on a concrete foundation. The need to minimize weight is not an issue, so rather than build a small stable, one could erect a standard 12ft × 10ft building in more or less the same way. And if you plan ahead and leave room for expansion, additional extensions such as a tack room and feed store can be added later.

The static stable must sit on a firm foundation. The site should be excavated to a hard subsoil, then filled with limestone rubble, and topped off with at least 4–5in (10–13cm) of concrete, leaving 2in (5cm) of foundation above ground level. To secure the wall panels to the foundation, very strong steel brackets are bolted to the lower horizontal rails, then 'rawlbolted' to the concrete using 'M8' rawlbolts.

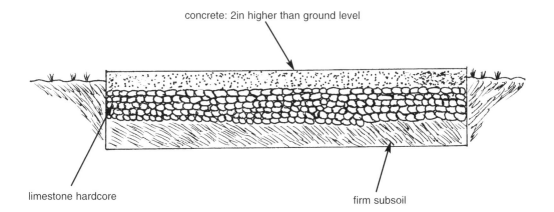

Concrete foundation for a static loosebox.

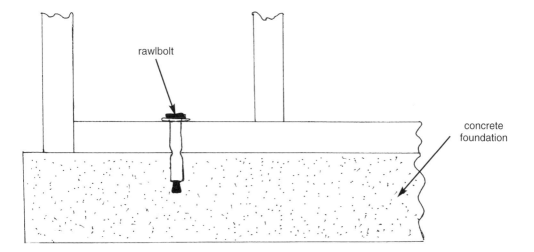

Fixing the wall panel to a foundation.

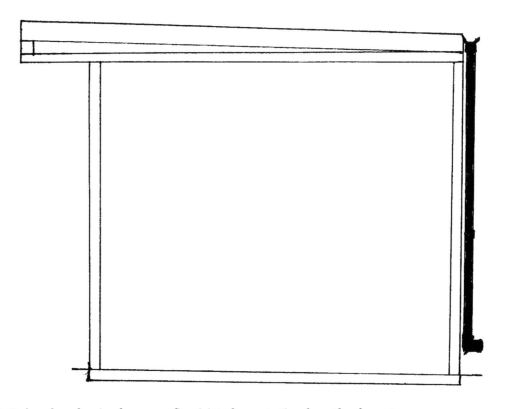

Static loosebox showing longer roofing joists for protection from the elements.

CHAPTER 6

BASIC CROSS-COUNTRY FENCES

Although general hacking is enjoyable just for its own sake, many riders want to compete – and what better for practice than a safe, well thought-out cross-country fence conveniently located at home. This chapter describes the construction of six easy-to-build jumps, suitable for novices.

Safety and good working practices are the priorities here. A poorly constructed or badly positioned obstacle is a potentially dangerous trap that could seriously injure both pony and rider; therefore it is essential to choose the most suitable materials and location. Your jump, no matter what form it takes, will benefit from being made out of strong, treated timber, because not only will it have to stand up to the rigors of nature and remain safe at all times, it will also need to cope with the constant, sometimes strong approaches of a horse or pony. A cross-country fence will, at some point, come into contact with an animal, especially if it is located in the animal's usual grazing paddock; this is an inevitable course of events. With this in mind, the jump should be free from sharp corners, large splinters, protruding metal fixings, and anything else that would cause potential harm. Furthermore, the obsta-cle must suit the rider it is intended for: there is little point in erecting a large fence suitable for confident riders, for example, when small novice children want to jump it.

The fences described below are all suitable for novices.

Materials and Tools

Some of the six fences described in this chapter will use different materials; however, the timber needs for each of the items are listed under their relevant subheadings, along with their specifications. With all the timber used, the common factors must be quality and suitability: it is not just the skill of the rider that gives the horse the confidence to tackle a demanding obstacle, it must also trust the safety of whatever you lay in its path. A flimsy contraption that looks easily collapsible is off-putting and potentially dangerous.

So what is suitable timber? This depends on the part of the jump under construction. Poles, for example, can be made of brand new, machine-rounded pine, substantial tree trunks, railway sleepers or old telegraph posts. Fillers can range from water containers and oil

All the poles on cross-country fences should be roped rather than nailed or bolted on. This next set of photographs shows, in detail, how to achieve this aim. Here: cutting the rope.

The second job is to tie a 'figure-of-eight' knot at one end of the rope.

Wrap the rope around the pole where it extends beyond the main uprights.

Whilst keeping hold of the figure-of-eight, pull the other end of the rope around the front of the main upright and under the pole.

Take the end of the rope around the back of the pole, then pull both ends tight to allow the pole to jam up against the post.

Feed the rope end through the figure-of-eight knot, pull it taught, and tie it off with a simple knot on the higher section.

Feed the rope end through the lower section.

Feed the rope end through the higher coil and back down through the lower section.

Pull it very tight until the two coils begin to close together. Continue like this until most of the rope is used.

The end of roping. Leave about 5in (13cm) of rope, and tie it off on one of the coils with a simple knot.

drums to finely constructed gates using treated, half-round or square rails. Generally it is better if a jump has a 'ground line', as this helps the horse to judge the obstacle.

The terrain will also play an important role where jump quality is concerned. A confident animal could approach an obstacle at speed, and this will call for a safe, level landing area on the other side, with ample room for the horse to stride forward and turn safely. The field containing the jumps should allow space for a straight, well-sighted approach, a comfortable take-off, and a smooth landing. The use of nails and screws must be avoided, and the only acceptable metal fixings are fencing staples and wire for joining 'governors' to uprights. A 'governor' is used for bracing the back of a jump, and is usually made out of fencing stakes; all cross-country fences must have these.

The tools that are required – and these are mostly applicable to all the jumps discussed here – are as follows:

- Spade
- Crowbar
- Fencing pliers
- Fencing maul
- Post slammer
- Claw hammer
- Tape measure
- High-lift jack (optional for lifting heavy poles)
- Hacksaw and metal file, or angle grinder
- Spirit level
- Power drill, rechargeable drill, or manual brace
- Powered or manual auger (optional)
- Powered sander, rechargeable sander, or surform-rasp

Health and Safety

- Steel toe-capped boots or wellingtons
- Leather working gloves
- Chainsaw safety clothing (*see* safety feature in Chapter 1)
- Waterproof clothing
- First-aid kit

- Chainsaw (*see* safety feature in Chapter 1) or hand saw

Basic Jump

The dimensions of this basic jump, suitable for novice horses and ponies and their riders, are 12ft × 2ft high (3.6m × 60cm). The materials that would be needed for its construction are listed below:

- 2 × 4ft × 8in (1.2m × 20cm) diameter, unpointed posts
- 1 × 12ft × 6in (3.6m × 15cm) diameter pole
- 4 × 4ft × 3.5in (1.2m × 9cm) pointed fencing stakes
- Single-strand fencing wire
- 12ft (3.6m) of rope
- Fencing staples

Putting in the Upright Posts

After deciding on an appropriate site (take advice from an expert if necessary), begin by excavating one posthole to a depth of 2ft (60cm). Firm the post in using tamped soil only, and adjust it with the spirit level. Next, take the 12ft (3.6m) pole and lay it on the ground, against the upright. Move the pole to the line you wish the jump to take, and place a marker on the ground. Dig a second posthole and firm in

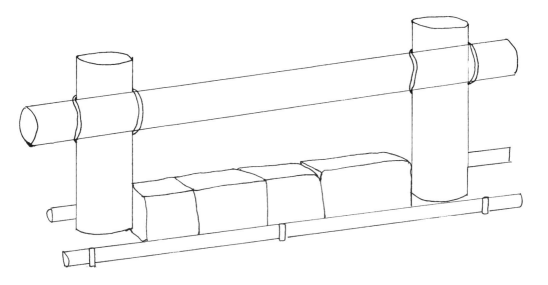

Basic jump with barrel ground line.

the other post. With the two uprights standing firm, adjust the pole until there is an even overhang at both ends.

With the maul, drive in the two 4ft (1.2m) fencing stakes, in front of the uprights, on the approach side of each post (the side of the jump that faces the oncoming horse and rider). These are going to act as chocks for the top pole, and will need to be trimmed at least 6in (15cm) below the height of the main uprights. The latter measurement represents the diameter of our pole, so the amount you trim from the stake will depend on the size of timber used. Working on the other side of the uprights, drive in two further stakes, to act as governors, and saw these to the level of the jump.

All the posts should be wired together, and you should do this as follows: cut two 4ft lengths of fencing wire. Then, working from the landing side of the jump, attach one end of the wire using one fencing sta-

ple driven home. Wrap the rest of the wire around the main upright and onto the governor. Tension the wire with the fencing pliers, and whilst holding this tension, hammer in another staple. Lastly, bring the wire back round to the starting point, tension it, and fix it with a staple. Trim off any excess, and embed the sharp ends into the timber. Repeat this for the next set of stakes.

Lifting on the Jump Pole

Next, the main pole must be lifted on and, depending on the materials used, you may need some sort of lifting gear, or at least another person to help you. Carefully lift the pole onto the chocks, and adjust it until the overhang at each end is the same. As a safety measure, to stop the pole from rolling off, it can be temporarily braced with a stake, placed at an angle with the ground. Lastly, cut

A fencing staple, driven home, locks the end of the wire to the back of the main upright.

Tensioning the wire against the governor.

The wire is stapled to the governor whilst the fencing pliers maintain the tension.

The wire is taken around the governor, then tensioned back onto the main upright.

After stapling, the free wire ends are trimmed with wire cutters.

Fencing staples are used to cover the sharp wire ends.

three 4ft (1.2m) lengths of rope and tie the pole onto each upright (refer to the illustrations for roping off at the beginning of this chapter).

Installing the Ground Line

Finally, the ground line on the approach side of the obstacle must be installed. This may be a half-round fencing rail laid on the ground, braced at each end with a couple of small stakes. To make the jump more interesting, a row of identical water containers can be used to simulate a 'filler'; though if you are going to do this, they must be secured at ground level to stop them being blown away or kicked out of place. Again, this may take the form of a rail placed on each side of the containers and braced with stakes.

Using a chainsaw or hand saw, trim the top of the main uprights level with the pole, being careful not to slice through the ropes. Round off all the sharp edges and corners with a surform-rasp or sander, and run a gloved hand over the entire structure to check for anything abnormal that might cause injury.

Finishing Off

To complete the project, dispose of any waste matter, inspect the ground for stray nails and staples, and check (and re-check) the obstacle for hazardous splinters and sharp metal ends.

Tyre Jump

The tools you will need to make this jump are the same as were used for the basic jump. The materials that are required are as follows:

- 6 × 4ft × 6in (1.2m × 15cm) unpointed posts
- 1 × 12ft × 6in (3.6m × 15cm) diameter pole
- 4 × 18in × 3.5in (46cm × 9cm) rails (for use as batons)
- Enough car tyres to fill between the main uprights (the number you need will depend on the width of the tyres)
- Single-strand fencing wire
- Fencing staples
- 6in (15cm) galvanized nails
- A selection of large stones for packing the uprights

The height of the tyre jump is governed by the size of the tyres used. For the obstacle to function effectively, the tyres should be touching the ground whilst at the same time hanging on the pole in order to produce a solid feature.

Method of Construction

The main frame of the tyre jump takes the same form as the basic jump, and the main uprights should be inserted as described for that obstacle. For added stability, however, both the governor and 'chock' stakes can be left higher than the main uprights, thus forming a slot into which the jump pole may be inserted. The tyres should be threaded onto the pole, and the pole positioned on the uprights. Once the pole is in position, complete with tyres, it should be tied on as described for the basic jump. Make the jump even more secure by placing a rail on the ground on each side, braced with stakes, in the same way as the 'filler' containers were made secure on the basic jump; this will prevent the tyres being knocked out of place if a horse or pony were to touch them whilst jumping.

An example of a tyre jump.

The Natural Brush Jump

Many cross-country jumps are designed to represent natural obstacles of the countryside, such as streams, hedges, banks, ditches and gates. However, since most of the rural landscape is privately owned, the chances of being able to gallop and jump beyond the confines of your land are limited, unless you go to an organized event. But with natural obstacles, to some extent you can bring this excitement home. Perhaps the best known and easiest to build is the brush jump, not only aesthetically pleasing, but still one

of the safest, and yet a thoroughly challenging fence. You will need the following materials:

- 4 × 12ft × 6in (3.6m × 15cm) half-round rails
- 2 × 4ft × 8in (1.2m × 20cm) posts
- Rope or wire to bind the brush filling of the jump
- Rope for tying on poles (as described for the basic jump)
- A generous selection of brush

When choosing suitable brush, always cut near the end of a branch to ensure a

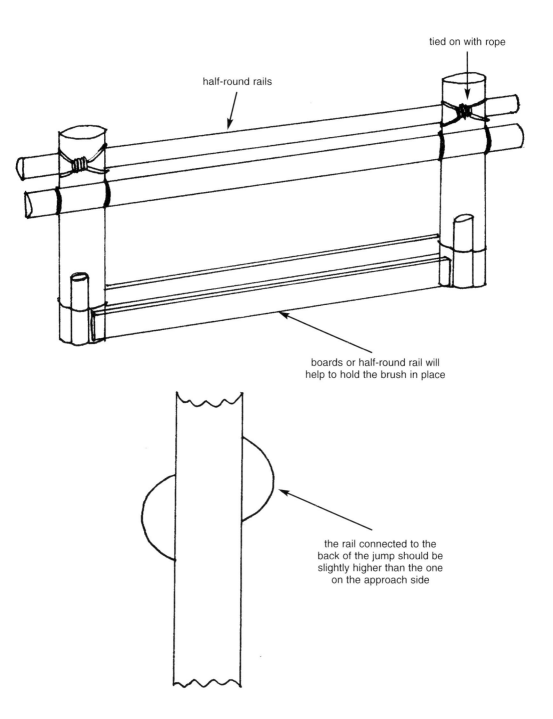

tied on with rope

half-round rails

boards or half-round rail will
help to hold the brush in place

the rail connected to the
back of the jump should be
slightly higher than the one
on the approach side

The frame for a brush jump.

A full brush jump. Note how the half-round support rails are roped on.

trunk of small diameter. Do not disturb trees during the nesting season; besides, in most cases it is an offence to damage trees in the wild or on public land. If the trees are growing on your own land it is far more beneficial to clip species that require thinning anyway. Another way of finding off-cuts is to approach a local tree surgeon or a local authority: both perform tree maintenance work, and they may be only too pleased for you to take away such waste.

Be aware that many species of tree and bush are poisonous to equines: avoid using oak, yew, laburnum, privet, laurel and rhododendron. The species commonly used for filling brush jumps is the *leylandii*, but even this can be toxic. To be on the safe side, steer clear of all ornamental garden flora, as many trees are unsuitable, even though they are non-poisonous; these include the thorny family such as hawthorn and buckthorn. It makes sense only to insert the 'brush' when you intend actually using the jump, and to remove it when animals are grazing around the jump – especially greedy ponies.

You will need the same tools as for the basic jump.

Method of Construction

Working to the same method as for the basic jump, excavate two postholes; remember to leave an overhang for the rails on each side before firming in the posts. Take two half-round rails and attach them to the top of the posts, one on each side, leaving the posts about 2in (5cm) proud; this you can trim off later. Next, affix the last two rails on each side of the jump, leaving a gap of 8in (20cm) between the top and the bottom cross-rails, to ensure against an animal trapping a hoof. Secure all the rails with rope, as described for the basic jump. As this jump may be used without brush, the back rail should be slightly higher than the front, so the horse has a clear view of the width of the obstacle.

With a chainsaw or hand saw, trim off the uprights to the same level as the top rails. Before inserting the branches, check the entire structure for hazards, then smooth all sharp corners with a surform-rasp or power sander.

To give the jump a tidy appearance, and to make sure the infill isn't dislodged in the wind, you should pack the brush tightly. To accomplish this, insert the branches until at least 4ft (1.2m) of the obstacle is full. Next, wrap a rope around the brush in 'U' fashion, leaving two ends clear of the main uprights. Stand at the side of the jump, holding both ends of the rope, and pull them towards you: this will have the effect of gathering the brush and compressing it inside the four cross-rails. Repeat this method until the jump is full.

If the top branches appear uneven, you can tidy them in the same way one would trim a hedge. As a last measure, check for sharp branches that may be standing proud of the top cross-rails.

It might sound like a good idea to plant trees inside the jump's frame to create a permanent hedge, but as trees mature their trunks increase in size, so this is not recommended.

The 'Coffin'

The combination fence known as a 'coffin' is a very challenging addition to any cross-country course. It consists of three obstacles: a basic rail, then a ditch, then another short distance to a second rail. If you have limited space then this is

---

Safety note

A new 'coffin' fence cannot be used until the loose soil around this ditch-and-rail combination fence has had time to firm up. This usually happens when the vegetation has been naturally reinstated around the obstacle.

---

probably not a complex of jumps you should consider. The distance between each obstacle should allow the horse or pony to land and stride comfortably to the next element; for a large horse the stride is around 26ft (8m), for a small pony it is about 20ft (6m). If pony and horse are sharing the jump, then the stride distance should be set at 26ft. Taking the width of the coffin ditch into account, at 2ft (0.6m), the total length of the jump complex will come to 54.5ft (16.6m).

Even if space is somewhat limited in your paddock, if you can fit in a combination like this somewhere, it will be of great advantage in building up the confidence of animal and rider, as it is just this type of obstacle that causes the most problems in competitions.

The following materials will be needed:

- 4 × 4ft × 6in (1.2m × 16cm) unpointed posts
- 2 × 12ft × 6in (3.6m × 16cm) poles
- 16 × 5ft × 3.5in (1.5m × 9cm) pointed fencing stakes
- 8 × 2ft × 2in × 2in (60cm × 5cm × 5cm) square pointed stakes. These are for creating a temporary string template. Metal pins or some other form of small ground stake could be used.
- 2 × 12ft × 6in (3.6m × 16cm) half-round rails or full round rails
- 2 × 10ft × 6in × 1.5in (3m × 16cm × 4cm) treated boards
- Fencing wire
- Rope
- Fencing staples

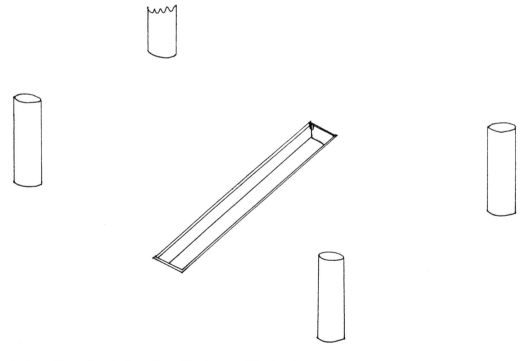

A three-dimensional view of a coffin jump without poles.

It is essential that you site the coffin-jump complex on flat, hazard-free land. The only complications a pony needs here are the obstacles themselves; loose boulders, divots and hillocks will only cause potentially dangerous problems. Even small stones might cause an accident, as could branches and other loose debris.

Measuring Out

Begin construction by measuring the total length of the combination. Lay a pole (pole A) on the ground, in the exact position it would be when forming part of the complex, and measure the 54.5ft (16.6m) to what will be the next rail. Lay the second pole (pole B) on this mark.

To align the jumps accurately, measure the distance between the ends of the poles A and B. It is better for the horse if you can construct the jumps parallel with each other. A sure way of doing this is to measure the diagonals from the left end of pole A to the right end of pole B, and vice versa. If the two are the same, the poles are true and parallel. Put a marker at each of the four points to represent the centre of the main uprights.

Both of the 'pole' obstacles within the coffin jump are built using all the techniques described for the basic jump, but a thorough inspection of all measurements should be carried out on a regular basis – including the distance between pole A and pole B.

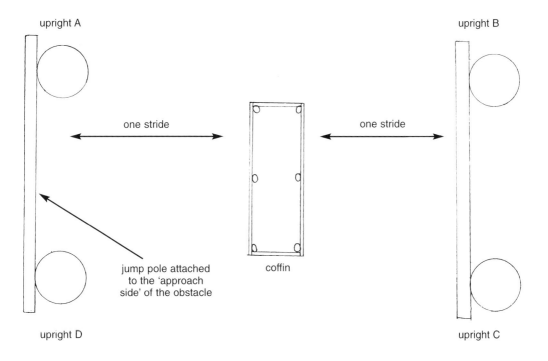

The coffin jump.

The last part of the jump is the 'coffin' ditch, and, like the poles, this must be correctly aligned. These next measurements are based on the size of the main uprights; they will not be the same if a different diameter post is used, and will only work if the two poles are aligned exactly. To position the coffin a 10ft × 2ft (3m × 60cm) string template should be set up to ensure accuracy. In addition to this, the correct 26ft (8m) equine stride will have to be maintained on both sides. Take a measurement of 6in (15cm) from the inside of each upright, and drive in a small marker stake at each of the four points.

Next, tie two strings to the marker stakes near upright 'A', and run them up to the markers near upright 'B'. Repeat this for uprights 'C' and 'D'. Pull the strings tight and tie them on. Both string lines should now be parallel. Working at upright A, measure 26ft down the string towards the middle element, and drive in another marker. Repeat this for the second stake on upright B. Use the same steps to line up the coffin from uprights C and D. With the four marker stakes in position, wrap a string line around them to form a rectangle.

Digging Out the Coffin Ditch

The exercise described above will have helped to make the 10ft × 2ft template for the coffin. The next job is to excavate the coffin using the string line as a guide for the edges of the trench. The coffin's depth must represent the width of the boarding, which will be installed a little later (*see* below); in our case this is 6in. It is also good practice to make the trench slightly larger than the template to make sure the wooden frame slots inside easily. When the

trench is complete, harden the base by walking up and down inside, then compact the sides to firm in any loose soil or stone.

With the coffin trench complete, it will now require some form of protection against collapse due to the continual pounding of hoofs that it will inevitably receive. This can be accomplished by using the 10ft boarding as an internal revetment. Start by dropping in the two 10ft boards, positioning them one on each side of the channel, then slide in two 2ft pieces of board at both ends. Using a lump hammer or fencing maul, drive in a small marker stake at each inside corner; stop when they are level with the board tops.

Working with both 10ft boards, now measure 5ft (1.5m) from the corners, and mark this distance on the individual board centres. Drive in another two stakes at these points. With a power or hand drill, pre-drill two nail holes through all of the stakes, though try to avoid piercing the boards on the other side. Attach the stakes to the boarding by driving in 6in nails. The nail points should now be sticking out on the opposite side; this is normal. To further strengthen the coffin, clench their shanks 90 degrees with the hammer until they are clasped tightly against the wood. The last procedure ensures that the stakes will stay in position if they are knocked or kicked. Lastly, fill the back of the boards with soil to the level of the surrounding ground. Please note, this jump should not be used until this soil has regenerated.

The project is complete after all timber features have been inspected for hazards, and all sharp edges have been smoothed over with a surform-rasp or power sander.

Adding extra, challenging features can further enhance the coffin fence, based on the same construction principles just described. You could, for example, lay containers under the poles, or even add some sturdy, half-round rail to the lower part of the uprights. Fill the coffin with wood shavings to make it more 'spooky' for the horse, and thus pose an additional challenge.

Stile Jump

The minimum width of this jump is 6ft (1.8m). The stile jump is a reproduction of a wooden step-over stile found on public footpaths all over the countryside. Due to its narrow width it is one of the more challenging cross-country fences.

The governors are driven in against the stile's loose uprights. Next they are wired together.

Roping on the stile's half-round rail.

The completed stile jump.

Materials and Tools

- 2 × 6ft × 6in (2m × 15cm) unpointed posts
- 4 × 4ft × 3in (1.2m × 8cm) round stakes
- 2 × 3ft × 6in (90cm × 15cm) unpointed posts (for the mock stile tread uprights)
- 1 × 2ft × 6in (1.2m × 15cm) half-round rail (for the mock stile tread)
- 1 × 8ft × 6in (2.4m × 15cm) half-round rail
- Fencing wire
- Fencing staples

The following tools will be required:

- Spade
- Crowbar
- Fencing maul or post slammer

The stile jump in action.

- Fencing pliers
- Claw hammer
- Chainsaw or hand saw
- Surform-rasp or power sander
- Spirit level
- Tape measure

Method of Construction

Using the method for the basic jump, construct the main stile's frame, including uprights, governors and chocks. Instead of sawing the main uprights to the level of the pole, leave their heights as they are. This will add to the challenge of the jump. The mock tread uprights and tread should be inserted 2ft apart underneath the cross pole, preferably near the centre point of the obstacle. To avoid the tread becoming a hazard, inset the uprights diagonally so that most of it is under the pole. Place the 2ft section of half-round so that it bridges both tread uprights, and secure it to the uprights using wire and staples. The stile treads will also double as a ground line, so there is no need to place anything else on the ground.

A row of water containers can make an interesting and simple obstacle. The two uprights at each end help to secure the containers.

Other Interesting Features

To create a decent obstacle does not really require the backbreaking work of digging holes: simple features on the ground will prove adequate, especially to the novice and beginner. For example, with the addition of two supporting posts (or braces) driven in at each end, the containers mentioned in the basic jump can become an obstacle in their own right. Another variation of this type of jump is a row of old steel drums; and to take this idea one stage further, the simple addition of a telegraph pole sited on the ground and braced with small stakes will make the fence more taxing.

Try this one out for an idea: a row of flowers or fruit, placed in line, can form a light-hearted, tricky jump. It may not sound tricky, but wait until the pony realizes it's there – especially one with a hearty appetite!

You might also be able to take advantage of the natural terrain to create interesting obstacles – indeed, natural features quite often play an important part in cross-country competitions. It may be that you already have an area on your land that can pose a demanding trial for horse and rider; for instance, the most common natural obstacle you will find on many cross-country courses is water. Natural, shallow streams containing a firm bed are an ideal test of horse and rider ability – though the stream bed will have to be free from loose rocks and boulders, and the entry and exit points should

Ground rails are placed on both sides and held in place by small stakes, further adding to the obstacle's security.

A sawn-down telegraph pole, held in position by fencing stakes, can make a simple cross-country obstacle.

A natural stream can make an ideal cross-country obstacle.

consist of a gentle slope, and not a vertical drop.

Another common feature is a gateway through to a neighbouring field. Sometimes this is just a gate to open and close, but a more interesting barrier is a slip rail. Slip rails are, as their name suggests, removable sections of timber that are inserted between four stakes, and can easily be 'slipped' out to provide a way through, either from one field to another, or as a purpose-built rail for competitors in hunter trials. The accompanying photograph shows just how easy slip rails are to build.

Slip rails can easily be 'slipped' out for easy access. When closed they act as a barrier against livestock.

BUILDING A BASIC SHOW JUMP

Most riders at some point in their lives will have the chance to jump competitively, even if it is just in a 'clear round' ring, and having the opportunity to practise at home will enhance their performance at competitions. A show jump is made up of four parts: two stands, usually called wings, a pole and a filler. Owning just one pair of wings can offer the rider many interesting scenarios, depending on the filler used. A filler can be anything from a coloured board, to a brush to a fake brick wall: the possibilities are an endless demand on one's imagination. Having two fences will increase the range of challenges, as the rider can then practise negotiating doubles and turns.

Safety is of paramount importance to both pony and rider, and an incorrectly assembled obstacle has the potential to cause serious injury. Wings must be constructed with a high centre of gravity so they fall relatively easily when pushed; and fillers must sit in shallow, preferably factory-made jump cups so they can fall away without hurting the animal. Every inch of the filler and wings must be 'equine friendly', with no sharp edges and no protruding metal bolts. Generally the wings' feet should be detachable, but this is more of a construction issue than a safety requirement, because most of the stress and wear occurs around the lower section. Permanent, fixed feet will eventually break off, sometimes beyond repair.

The project described in this chapter is for a 5ft (1.8m)-high set of wings. To minimize their weight, both will taper down to a height of 2ft (60cm). The overall length of each wing will be 3ft (or 1m), with the intermediate rails fixed in 'fan' fashion to give the finished article an ornate look. The materials for the jump can be purchased from most agricultural retailers and sawmills with a retail outlet.

Materials and Tools

Please note that the sizes of timber given relate to the vital statistics of the book's project show-jump. Most sizes of timber are sold in standard lengths and may have to be purchased as such. You will need the following materials:

- 1 × 10ft × 4in × 2in (3m × 10cm × 5cm) square rail (for the front uprights)
- 1 × 4ft × 3in × 2in (1.2m × 7cm × 5cm) section of square rail (for the rear uprights)
- 3 × 12ft × 3in × 1in (3.6m × 7cm ×

2.5cm) square rail (for the frame construction)
- 1 × 8ft × 2in × 6in (2.4m × 7cm × 15cm) section of boarding (for the feet)
- Nuts and bolts (for constructing the wings)
- Threaded bar, complete with nuts and bolts (for attaching the feet)
- 1.5in (38mm) screws (for constructing the wings)

- 4 × metal, pre-drilled back plates (to help attach the feet); if these are hard to find, another method is described later in the chapter

You will need the following tools:

- Electric or rechargeable drill
- Rechargeable screwdriver or drill
- Hammer or rubber mallet

The type of materials required to make two show-jump wings.

- Spanners or socket set
- Tape measure
- Hacksaw or grinder
- Hand saw (a jigsaw will come in handy when shaping the jump's feet)
- A file suitable for smoothing metal; a grinder can be used in its place
- Surform rasp or sander for smoothing sharp edges

Ideally the show jump should be constructed in a workshop, using a firm work surface, but acceptable results can be achieved outside on hard, level ground. The first job is to separate the timbers. The 10ft × 4in rail is going to be used for the jump's main supports; this is the section that holds the jump cups. The 3in × 2in rail is for the back supports, and the 12ft × 3in × 1in rails are for the intermediate braces, the part of the jump that gives it shape and appearance.

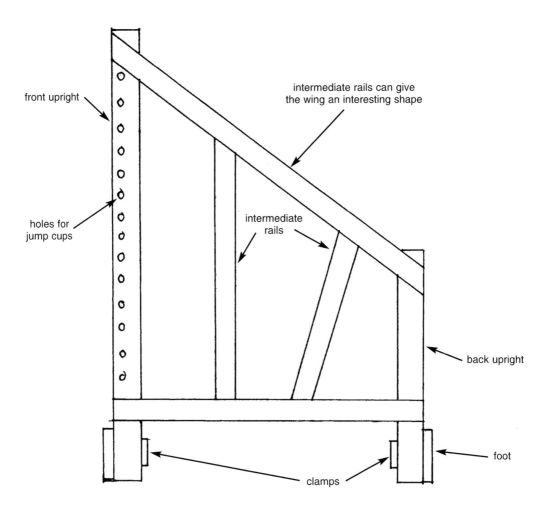

front upright

intermediate rails can give the wing an interesting shape

holes for jump cups

intermediate rails

back upright

foot

clamps

Parts of a show-jump wing.

Constructing a Wing

Begin by sawing the 10ft × 4ft rail into two equal 5ft (1.5m) lengths, and place them to one side. Next, make two 2ft (60cm) timbers from the 10ft × 3in × 2in rail, and store them next to the main supports. Take one of the 12ft × 3in rails, and measure and cut two 3ft timbers.

Take one of the 5ft supports and one 2ft back support, then measure 8–10in (20–25cm) from their bottoms (the bottom of each support will touch the ground, and will not be seen when the feet are connected). If your sawing was not accu-rate, it is a good idea to use these rough cuts as the base, not for constructional reasons, but merely for looks. Working from the bottom of the uprights, measure 8–10in towards the top. Mark this mea-surement using a set square, or another accurate guide. Ensure the measure-ments are the same on both timbers.

Taking one of the 3ft rails, lay it paral-lel to the marks, making sure both ends are flush with the outside edges of the uprights. This bottom rail will eventually be bolted to the show jump, but as a tem-porary holding method they should be screwed in place; one screw at either end will suffice.

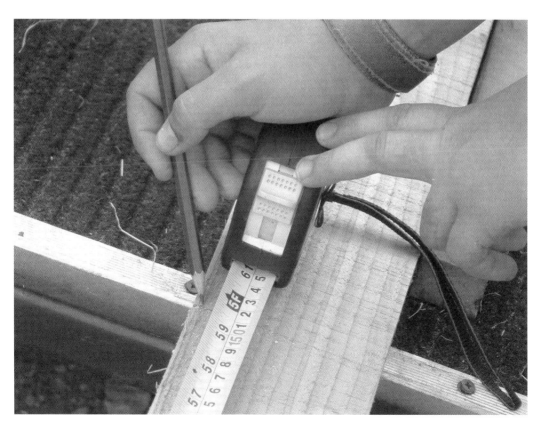

Measuring the 5ft (1.5m) mark on the main uprights.

The two 5ft uprights after sawing.

Using a hand saw to draw the straight line at the 5ft mark.

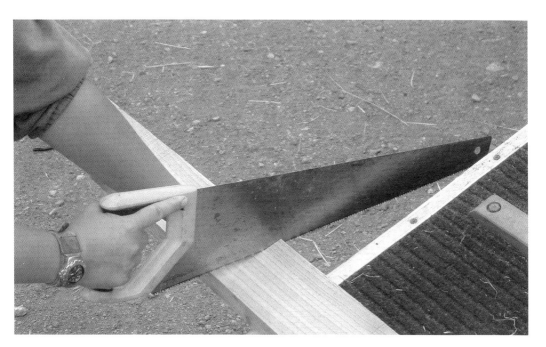

Sawing the 10ft × 4in × 2in rail into two 5ft lengths.

Measuring and marking the 8in (20cm) for the wing's lower cross-rail.

Making sure the two uprights are parallel.

Working just above the rail, establish the distance between both uprights then, using this measurement as a guide, adjust the top of the back upright against the main front one. The two uprights should be exactly parallel. It is important not to disturb this gap; doing so could upset the balance and look of the show jump. The ideal way to ensure that the correct distance is maintained is to clamp the rails on, minimizing any movement. Using the remaining 6ft section of rail, carefully place it on the frame, ensuring an overlap either side of the jump. Before screwing this rail into place, recheck the measurement between the front and back timbers, and adjust if needed.

The wing is now rigid enough to be moved. The next step is to drill a hole through each corner of the wing; these are for the nuts and bolts that hold the frame together. The drill holes must be as close to the centre of the uprights as possible to prevent splitting and to avoid future weakness. Drilling completely through timber can cause unsightly splitting when the bit pierces the other side. You can avoid this to a certain degree by laying the timber on some old rail and allowing the bit to cut into this on its journey through.

Before inserting bolts, recheck the gap between the two uprights, and adjust if required. With the wing still in position

The wing uprights with the bottom rail at the 8in (20cm) mark.

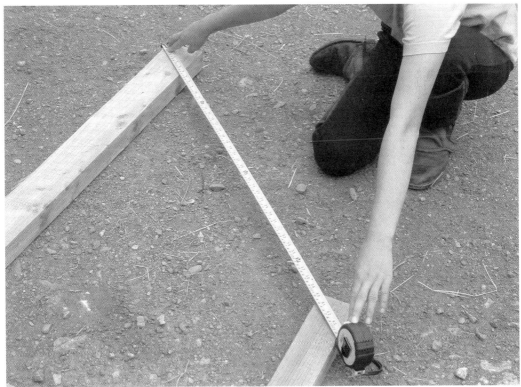

Measuring for the top rail. Make sure you add an extra 2in for trimming off at either end.

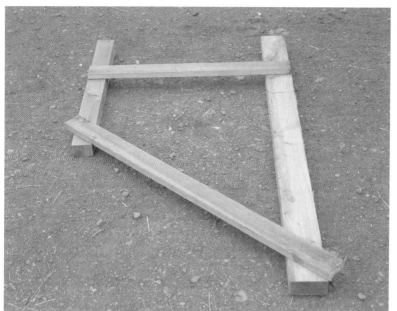

The wing with its top rail.

Affixing the rails to the uprights with screws.

on the ground, gently drive the four bolts through the holes using either a mallet or hammer. Be careful, at this point, not to push them all the way, especially if you are working on a hard surface such as concrete: doing so could spoil the threads, making it difficult to screw nuts on later. When the bolts are inserted, stand the wing up, holding it firmly whilst gently driving them home. Finally the washers and nuts can be attached, then tightened with a spanner or suitable-sized socket.

Now that the basic frame has been constructed, the intermediate rails can be affixed. We built the project jump for this book using two rails: one was attached vertically, and the other offset at a slight angle to give the obstacle a more interesting, fan-like appearance. How one places these rails is a matter of choice, but the gaps between each timber should be not less than 4in (10cm), but no wider than 8in (20cm), otherwise you risk trapping a horse's or pony's hoof. Each timber should be fixed with four screws, two at each end (after pre-drilling to avoid splitting the rail). Before making the feet, any overhanging timber should be sawn flush with the jump.

Making the Feet

Although the feet are the smallest part of a show jump, they do play a very

Pre-drilling at each corner for the wing's nut and bolts.

Gently driving the bolts through the rails and uprights with a hammer or mallet.

Driving the bolts home.

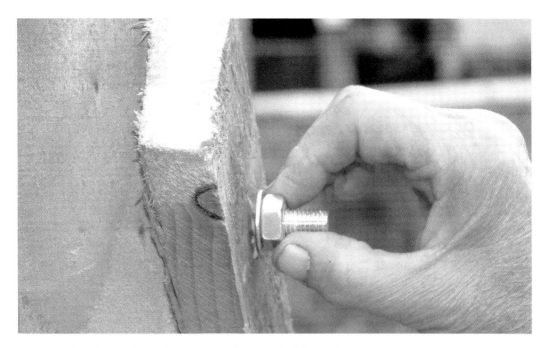

After adding the washers, the nuts are then hand tightened.

Locking down the nuts with a ratchet and socket.

important role. The size of the feet is critical to the stability of the jump: the wings of a jump must be stable enough to remain upright even when the pole or filler is knocked down by the jumping horse; but if the horse falls against them they should knock over. Thus, if the feet are too long they will not fall over easily; but if they are too small, the jump will be top heavy and may topple over at the slightest touch.

Also important is how the feet are actually secured to the wings. Screwing or bolting them directly to the frame is risky, because should the feet become displaced, the fixings may be exposed, or the damage to the wood will cause sharp splinters, and obviously this has the potential to cause considerable injury.

Show-jump feet should therefore be made as a separate entity, able to come away in one piece when the need arises. The following describes a method that can achieve this.

For a 5ft-high jump wing, similar to our project obstacle, feet of between 18–24in (45–60cm) long should give adequate stability. Working with 2in × 6in board, measure and saw four 2ft (0.6m) sections. The corners at the top of the feet should be sawn away with either a hand saw or a jigsaw. On the project jump, as you can see from the photographs, we cut away a substantial amount of timber from the top corner of each of the feet. There is no hard and fast rule as to the shape of the feet; what is important here is to lose the sharp corners on all the top edges.

After sawing the board into 2ft (60cm) lengths, the top corners of each foot are then measured and sawn. The pencil is just to highlight the angle.

The next job is to drill the feet so that the threaded rod can be inserted in order to help secure them to the wings. If you are using pre-drilled, steel back-plates, they should be placed in a central position on each foot and used as a template for the drill holes. With a pencil, draw around the inside of the back-plates' holes, onto the timber, then mark the centres ready for drilling. Depending on the diameter of threaded rod purchased – our rod was 10mm – a matching, or slightly wider twist drill bit should be used for drilling into the feet.

It is now time to saw the threaded rod. For the time being, the rods should be 2in (5cm) greater in length than the uprights and their corresponding feet when placed together. For example, if the width of the upright is 4in, and the thickness of the feet is 2in, each rod should be 8in (20cm) long.

Next, attach nuts and washers to each of the rod ends, and twist them down until at least 0.5in (1cm) of thread is showing. Push the rods through the jump's feet, then place the feet against both uprights, ensuring that the nuts and washers are on the outward face. Next, insert the steel plates over the opposite ends of the rods and push them against the back of the upright. Lastly, place a washer and nut on each bare rod end, and turn them tightly with a spanner or socket until the back plates clamp both uprights.

If steel back plates cannot be found, then you could create your own with the

Clamping the foot to the wing with a wooden back plate and threaded rod.

The finished foot before smoothing off the sharp edges.

offcuts of rail. The principle of securing them to the feet is the same, but they can be high maintenance and will not last as long their steel counterparts. As an example for this book, the project jump contained both steel and wooden back plates. The latter is still a safer alternative than affixing directly to the wings' uprights.

A show jump is no use unless it can hold jump cups to rest poles on; thus the next phase of the job is to drill a series of accurately spaced holes through the 5ft uprights, to take a jump cup's locking pin. To do this freehand may sound like a daunting task, but it really couldn't be easier. Both wings each contain fourteen 12mm holes, their centres evenly spaced at 3in apart; a uniform line is easily achieved by working down the outside edges of the large uprights with a tape

measure. At regular intervals along the upright's 4in face, measure 1.5in towards the centre. With a long straight-edge aligned against these marks, scribe a pencil line from top to bottom. Using the tape again, and working from bottom to top, draw a mark every 3in along this line. These will be the centres for the drill holes. With a 12mm auger or twist-drill bit inserted in an electrical drill or manual brace, drill out the fourteen holes.

The last phase of the job is to smooth down all corners and edges, paying particular attention to the nuts and bolts. A grinder with a suitable disk is ideal for this, as it can be used to round off the sharp ends of the metal. Each bolt that faces outwards (towards the direction of horse and rider) must be ground flush with its nuts. The only bolts that should

Drilling the holes for the jump-cup pins.

remain slightly proud are the ones holding the back plates against the uprights on the inside. You will need some thread to facilitate the loosening of the bolts when removing the feet. Having said that, the ends of these bolts should be smoothed over.

With the first jump wing complete, all that remains to do is to construct the second. The construction method is exactly the same, except that this wing will be a mirror image of the first; the method will have to take that into account. It is a useful check to align both wings before drilling the jump cup holes in the second one, to ensure that the holes are level with each other; otherwise it will be impossible to make the jump pole straight.

Decorating the jump wings is a matter

Smoothing down the metalwork with a grinder.

The completed wings with jump cups and poles. The pole resting on the feet acts as the jump's ground line.

for personal taste; they can be colourfully painted, or stained to form a rustic jump. For the wings to hold poles, suitable jump cups can be purchased from most equine retailers, either over the counter or by mail order. Suitable timber for jump poles can be obtained at the outlets mentioned earlier in this book.

The finished show jump in action.

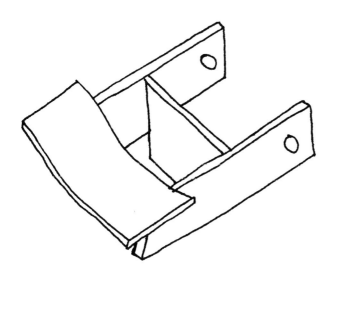

pin for insertion into wing

Galvanized jump cup.

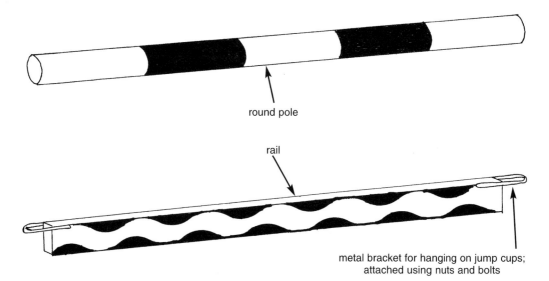

round pole

rail

metal bracket for hanging on jump cups; attached using nuts and bolts

all jump poles are 8ft (2.4m)

Examples of show jump poles.

CHAPTER 8

SOLUTIONS AND SAFETY

Even with the greatest care and the best working practices, the unpredictability of the equine temperament can lead to disaster within even the most unforeseen and, seemingly, benign circumstances. Experienced horse owners will tell you that what appears safe today could, in the blink of an eye, turn itself into an expensive vet's bill; with the best will in the world some things are almost impossible to predict. The incidents in this chapter are drawn from experience, with the first example describing an accident that could not have been anticipated, and could only have been avoided in retrospect.

Corrugated Hell

Galvanized, corrugated steel farm buildings are very common, they are cheap to erect, and at the same time very durable. The establishment described here has owned one of these buildings for many years, and it had been constantly maintained to a very high standard, along with the other stables and looseboxes. No one could have foreseen what was about to happen. The open-fronted steel building, used to store hay, also had two looseboxes contained within it, and not one injury had ever been sustained during its many years of accommodating drinking, eating and resting equines; it had also been used as a foaling box on many occasions.

The incident in question involved an expensive mare that sustained a potentially life-threatening injury. The animal's temperament was volatile at the best of times, but it had used this particular building for some years without mishap. According to the owners, whilst the mare was lying down she had kicked out with her hind legs, perhaps in temper or whilst rolling, and her hoofs had smashed against the metal walls. This in itself was astonishing, as a 3ft (1m) high breezeblock plinth, designed to take the brunt of an impact just such as this, supported the building.

But in kicking with such force the horse had managed to get a leg wedged between a join of two corrugated sheets. In panic she had tried to release herself, but this had only made the situation worse, and in her struggles the two metal sheets had acted like razor blades, cutting into the fetlock and eventually severing the tendon. How she managed to free herself is still a mystery, but the pain must have been unbearable. Having sustained considerable blood loss, the mare was discovered during the early morning, and the local horse vet was called out to deal with the emergency. In most cases an injury like this one is fatal. Thankfully, due to the skill of the vet and the loving attention of the mare's owners, she made a full recovery and is still ridden to this day.

I was called in the day after to repair the building. Rather than just rejoining the corrugated sheeting, I erected a 2ft (60cm) timber skin in front of the metal, which in effect raised the 'kicking area'. First I had to find a way of fixing the timber to the breezeblock, and managed to achieve this by bolting 12ft (3.6m) rails to the top of the wall and nailing the boarding onto this. Securing the top section was easy, as the building's supporting structure was made out of 3in × 2in (7.6 ×

5cm) timber batons, situated 2ft (60cm) above the breeze-block plinth.

Every situation is different, and whilst we can prepare for disasters, the unforeseen occurs all the time. Repairing this building was almost 'shutting the stable door after the horse has bolted'; but by taking steps to reduce the risks inherent in what had shown itself, in dramatic fashion, to be a potentially lethal hazard, the owner has prevented a reoccurrence of this type of injury to another horse.

That said, catastrophe is only avoided when it happens to someone else first, and it is through these experiences that lies the key to pre-empting such disasters in the future. For instance, I was very quick to board up a corrugated metal partition in my own stable straight after this incident.

The building before the wooden boards were installed.

The wooden boards hiding the metal sheeting.

Strong Walls and Breaking Doors

Many equestrian establishments, be they private or commercial, still stable their equine stock in old, purpose-built brick or stone buildings; and as long as their structural condition is maintained in good order, these can outlast generations of owners and animals. The fact that they are still standing today proves that point. Bricks and mortar will outlast wooden constructions, particularly when exposed to the elements. Timber window frames and, more importantly, door surrounds, and the doors themselves, will eventually require replacements, and the older the door, the more likely it is that it will require replacing. Window frames should

be attended to regularly, as serious injury could result should a window become damaged, and glass and debris perhaps showered into the stable. It is important that windows be kept in good repair, they should open inwards and upwards to encourage airflow, and ideally the horse should not be able to gain access to them, particularly if panes are of glass.

It is, however, the stable doors that sustain the most wear, whether through pushing, kicking or, as just mentioned, as a result of the onslaught of the elements. Couple this with the fact that if the building has not been maintained, the timber in these old doors will almost certainly be untreated, and probably bearing rusty tee-hinges as well as decaying screws; so

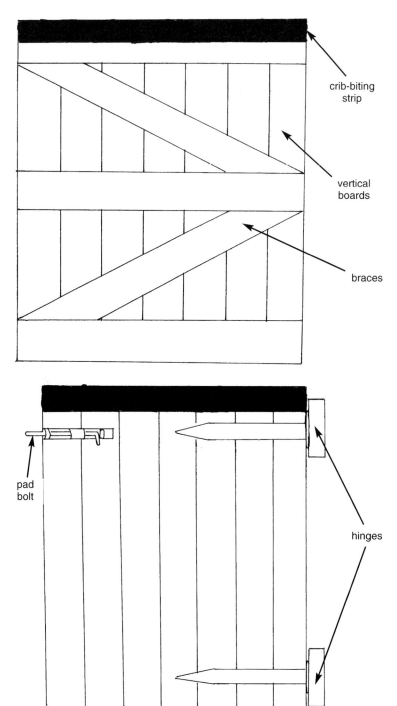

Parts of a stable door 'back'.

crib-biting strip

vertical boards

braces

pad bolt

hinges

Parts of a stable door 'front'.

the door won't stand much of a chance against a wilful animal.

The following project describes the construction of a new set of treated timber doors. The measurements given act only as a guide, because the door-frames on many old equine quarters can differ. The following specifications are based on the mobile loosebox constructed in Chapter 5. Ideally the door should be built on a solid, flat surface or a workbench.

Materials and Tools

You will need the following materials:

- For the bottom door: 11 × 4ft × 5in × 1in (1.2m × 12cm × 2.5cm) treated boards (two of these will be used for the door braces)
- 1 × 4ft × 3in × 1in (1.2m × 7.5cm × 2.5cm) treated board (an offcut of 12ft × 3in × 1in fencing rail is ideal)
- For the top door: 10 × 3ft × 5in × 1in (91cm × 12cm × 2.5cm) treated boards (4ft boards may have to be purchased)
- 1 × 3ft × 3in × 1in treated board
- 4 × 12in (30cm) galvanized T-hinges (these usually come with the correct screws)
- 1 × galvanized pad-bolt
- 2 sets of galvanized cabin hooks
- 1 × galvanized kick-over latch
- 1 box of 1.5in (38mm) pozidrive screws
- 1 galvanized crib-biting strip (cut to 43in (1.1m) in length)

You will need the following tools:

- Hand saw
- Power drill or rechargeable drill with screwdriver bits
- Tape measure
- Pencil

Method of Construction

Begin by laying seven of the vertical 4ft boards on a flat surface, side by side, slotting the thinner 3in board between the third and fourth. Adjust the timber until both ends are running flush. Next, take another 4ft board and lay it across the row, adjusting the upper edge until it is level with the top of the verticals; then join it to the 4fts by driving in two screws per vertical. Repeat the exercise for the bottom of the door.

The next job is to measure up for the central, horizontal timber. With the tape measure and pencil, place a mark at the 2ft point (the centre) on both edges of the door. Lay another 4ft board so that its ends are central to the markers. The board's centre is actually 2.5in. Affix it to the vertical boards, as described earlier.

For strength, all boarded doors should include diagonal braces that fit between the horizontal timbers. There are two ways for doing this: the complicated way and the easy way. The first method involves some arithmetic to ascertain the brace's actual length in relation to the door. The easy second technique is to simply lay one board diagonally across the verticals, from the top corner to the outside edge of middle timber. Then with a thin, straight vertical edge (such as a set square) jammed against the edge of the centre timber, scribe lines on both edges of the brace. On its 4in face, join these lines with the set square and pencil. To trim the board, saw down the marks you have just made, operating the saw as straight as possible. The brace should now fit in between the top and middle timbers. Use the sawn timber as a template for cutting the bottom brace, and affix both to the vertical boards with screws.

Because screws have been used to joined the timbers together, inspect the front and back of the door for possible protruding points. These should be cut off, bringing the fixing flush with the wooden boarding.

At the moment the top of the stable door is too narrow for the metal crib-biting strip, so the next job is to nail on a 43in length of 3in × 2in rail. This should be placed on the same side as the braces, and level with the top of the verticals.

Securing the Hinges

The door is now ready for the two T-hinges. These are secured to the front (the opposite side to the braces), one hinge per horizontal board. For the stable door to operate smoothly, the hinge plates (the part of the hinge that fixes to the door-frame) must run parallel with the vertical

Stable doors in their closed position with a full set of galvanized fixtures.

edge of the door, and the 'barrel' sections (the actual hinge parts) should be just be clear of the sides. Secure the hinges to the door with the screws provided.

The construction of the top door is more or less the same as the bottom, but there are a few slight differences. For instance, it need have only two horizontal top and bottom boards and a single, diagonal brace. An alternative timber is tongue and groove. This boarding will create a more aesthetically pleasing structure and be less prone to movement as a result of weathering.

Securing the Hooks

It is of vital importance that both doors can be secured in an open position, the bottom one for ease of coming in and out of the stable with a horse (to prevent the door blowing shut), and the top one for ventilation.

First, find the supporting brace of the door, then fix the loop part of the cabin hook to the front of the door, fixing the screws through the brace. Fix the hook to the stable wall, ensuring that both the loop and the hook are aligned. If the construction is of stone or brick, it will be necessary to drill into the wall and insert rawlplugs; then you can attach the fitting by screwing into the rawlplugs. Make sure that both bottom and top doors can be secured in this way.

Changing a Field Gate into a Bridle Gate

Bridle gates can be opened whilst the rider is mounted. In most circumstances,

Kick-bolts are fixed near the bottom of the door.

Some bored equines will persistently chew the top of stable doors: this is called crib-biting.

You can help deter crib-biting by adding a metal strip to the top of the stable door.

riders dismount, open the gate and walk the animal through. But what happens if the horse is difficult to mount, or the rider is unable to mount unaided? Operating a field gate with a standard 'auto latch' can sometimes prove awkward when trying to control an excited animal, and even more so when the latch is fixed to the opposite side. Replacing the auto latch with a bridle latch will solve this problem because it has a vertical mechanism that can be reached comfortably from both sides of the gate even when mounted.

Footpaths and Beefburgers

Paddocks that border public rights of way do have their drawbacks. People love to see horses and ponies happily roaming and grazing, and they will stop to look – and this in itself is no problem. Complications arise when, with all the best intentions, they treat the animal to snacks other than apples and carrots: thus beefburgers, cheese sandwiches, even fairy cakes have been offered to tempt the palate of my ponies.

There are a number of ways to help alleviate the problem. The first one is to put up a sign asking people not to feed the ponies – though unfortunately this sometimes encourages some contrary folk to feed them even more. The second is to install a secondary fence line, roughly 3ft from the boundary; an electric fence is the most cost-effective alternative, remembering that it is a statutory requirement to place a warning sign on electrified fencing close to public rights of way.

A bridle latch can be easily operated from both sides of the gate.

USEFUL ORGANIZATIONS

Related Statutory Organizations

Central Council of Physical Recreation
Francis House
Francis Street
London SW1P 1DE
Tel: 0207 828 3163/4
Fax: 0207 630 8820

Countryside Agency
John Dower House
Crescent Place
Cheltenham
Gloucestershire GL50 3RA
Tel: 01242 521381
Fax: 01242 584270

Countryside Council for Wales
Plas Penrhos
Fford Penrhos
Bangor
Gwynedd LL57 2LQ
Tel: 01248 370444

Deer Commission for Scotland
Knowsley
82 Fairfield Road
Inverness IV3 5LH
Tel: 01463 231751
Fax: 01463 712931

English Nature
Northminster House
Peterborough PE1 1UA
Tel: 01733 455000
Fax: 01733 568834

English Tourism Council
Thames Tower
Black's Road
London W6 9EL
Tel: 0208 563 3000
Fax: 0208 563 3234
email: comments@englishtourism.org.uk

Environment Agency
Rio House
Waterside Drive
Aztec West
Almondsbury
Bristol BS12 4UD
Tel: 01454 624400
Fax: 01454 624409

Forestry Commission
231 Corstorphine Road
Edinburgh EH12 7AT
Tel: 0131 334 0303
Fax: 0131 334 3047

USEFUL ORGANIZATIONS

Irish Sports Council
21 Fitzwilliam Square
Dublin 2

Joint Nature Conservation Committee
Monkstone House
City Road
Peterborough PE1 1JY
Tel: 01733 562626
Fax: 01733 555948

Scottish Natural Heritage
12 Hope Terrace
Edinburgh EH9 2AS
Tel: 0131 447 4784
Fax: 0131 446 2277

Sports Council
16 Upper Woburn Place
London WC1 0QP
Tel: 0207 273 1500

Sports Council for Northern Ireland
Tel: 028 90381222

Sports Council for Wales
Tel: 029 20300500

Sport Scotland
Tel: 0131 317 7200

UK Sport
Tel: 0207 841 9500
email: info@uksport.gov.uk

Related Equine Organizations

British Equestrian Federation
National Agricultural Centre
Stoneleigh Park
Kenilworth

Warks CV8 2RH
Tel: 024 7669 8871
Fax: 024 7669 6484

British Equestrian Vaulting
47 Manderley Close
Eastern Green
Coventry CV5 7NR
Tel: 024 7646 3027

British Eventing
National Agricultural Centre
Stoneleigh Park
Kenilworth
Warks CV8 2RN
Tel: 024 7669 8856
Fax: 024 7669 7235
email: info@britisheventing.com

British Show Jumping Association
National Agricultural Centre
Stoneleigh Park
Kenilworth
Warks CV8 2RJ
Tel: 024 7669 8800
Fax: 024 7669 6685
email: bsja@bsja.co.uk

Country Landowners Association
16 Belgrave Square
London SW1X 8PQ
Tel: 0207 235 0511
Fax: 0207 235 4696
email: mail@cla.org.uk

Countryside Alliance
The Old Town Hall
367 Kennington Road
London SE11 4PT
Tel: 020 7840 9200
Fax: 020 7793 8899
email: info@countryside-alliance.org

Equestrian Security Services (Freeze Marking)
17 St Johns Road
Farnham
Surrey GU9 8NU
Tel: 01252 727053
Fax: 01252 737738

Farriers Registration Council
Sefton House
Adams Court
Newark Road
Peterborough
Cambs PE1 5PP
Tel: 01733 319911
Fax: 01733 319910
email: frc@farrier-reg.gov.uk

Equine Grass Sickness Fund
The Moredun Foundation
Pentlands Science Park
Bush Loan
Penicuik
Midlothian EH26 0PZ
Tel: 0131 445 6257/5111
Fax: 0131 445 6235
email: equine@mf.mri.sari.ac.uk

Equine Behaviour Forum
Grove Cottage
Brinkley
Newmarket
Suffolk CB8 0SF
Tel: 01638 507502
Fax: 01772 786037
email: f.l.burton@udcf.glasgow.ac.uk

Guild of Master Craftsman
166 High Street
Lewes
East Sussex BN7 1XU
Tel: 01273 477374
Fax: 01273 478606
Contact: Information Officer

International League for the Protection of Horses
Anne Colvin House
Hall Farm
Snetterton
Norwich
Norfolk NR16 2LR
Tel: 01953 498682
Fax: 01953 498373

RSPCA
The Causeway
Horsham
West Sussex RH12 1HG
Tel: 01403 264181
Fax: 01403 241048
email: veterinary@rspca.org.uk

Society for the Welfare of Horses and Ponies
Coxstone
St Maughans
Monmouth NP5 3QF
Tel: 01600 750233
Fax: 01600 750468
email: swhp@swhp.co.uk

Welsh Trekking & Riding Association
118 Beacons Park
Brecon
Powys CF14 5GG
Tel: 01874 622521

National Association Farriers, Blacksmiths & Agricultural Engineers
Avenue B, 10th Street
National Agricultural Centre
Stoneleigh
Kenilworth
Warwickshire CV8 2LG
Tel: 024 7669 6595
Fax: 024 7669 6708
email: nafbae@nafbae.co.uk

National Equine Welfare Council
Stanton
10 Wales Street
Kings Sutton
Nr Banbury
Oxon OX17 3RR
Tel/Fax: 01295 810 060
email: newc@kingssutton.freeserve.co.uk

Pony Club
NAC Stoneleigh Park
Kenilworth
Warwickshire
CV8 2RW
email: enquiries@pcuk.org
Tel: 024 7669 8300
Fax: 024 7669 6836
Berwyn and Dee Branch
http://www.berwynanddee.co.uk

Pony Riders Association
22 Berry's Road
Upper Bucklebury
Reading
Berks RG7 6QN
Tel: 01635 867891

Open Spaces Society
25a Bell Street
Henley-on-Thames
Oxon RG9 2BA
Tel: 01491 573535

The Open College of Equine Science
Tel: 01284 700703
email: enquiries@equinestudies.co.uk

North Shropshire and Walford College
Baschurch
Shrewsbury
Shropshire SY4 2HL
Tel: 01939 262100

British Trust for Conservation Volunteers (BTCV)
36 St Mary's Street
Wallingford OX10 0EU
Tel: 01491 821600
The BTCV is Britain's largest conservation volunteer organization. It offers training courses on all aspects of practical countryside work, and has close relationships with local authorities, national parks and industry. Anyone who joins the BTCV has the opportunity to learn a wide range of practical skills such as stock fencing, drystone walling and more.

U K Wild News
http://www.ukwildnews.co.uk

Karen Czora Photos
http://www.czoraphotos.co.uk

GLOSSARY

Barbed wire: Pointed form of top wire used to deter large livestock from damaging fence lines. This should not be used for equine stock.

Bar strainer: A wire-straining tool ideal for tensioning barbed wire or straining the low-tensile wire on stock netting.

Cast-iron fencing maul: Very similar to a sledgehammer in looks, but designed for driving fencing stakes into the ground.

Chain strainer: Sometimes called a 'monkey' strainer. A tool for tensioning stock netting and top wire.

Cribbing: When a horse or pony chews the top of a stable door or fence.

Crowbar: Made from steel, and looks like a javelin. One end of the bar is pointed and ideal for starting postholes or breaking up hard ground, the other end usually comes with a chisel for splitting awkward stones or tree roots.

Drawbar: Part of the towing mechanism for trailers and mobile shelters.

Fencing pliers: A universal fencing tool with a grip for straining short sections of wire, a wire cutter, a hammer, a gouge for loosening fencing staples, and a pincer for pulling staples.

Fencing staple: A small 'U'-shaped fixing for attaching stock netting and top wire.

Field shelter: Three-sided or open-plan livestock accommodation, erected in fields and paddocks as sanctuary from the elements.

Kick board: Strong sheets of timber forming the inner wall of equine accommodation. Protects the building from damage by kicking.

Lick-over latch or *kick bolt*: A quick-release and quick-locking mechanism used on stable doors.

Loosebox: Accommodation for horses or ponies. Another word used to describe a stable.

Non-stock side: The side of the enclosure that faces away from the livestock; the other side of the fence.

Pad bolt: Very strong fastener, ideal for stable doors.

Post and rail fence: The most suitable form of equestrian enclosure.

Post auger: A petrol-powered or manual device designed to bore postholes.

Post slammer: A heavy duty, hollow, tubular device used for driving pointed fencing stakes.

Saddle rack: A steel shelving unit for storing saddles safely.

Slip rail: A strong fencing rail used as stock proofing when a cross-country jump, which forms part of a boundary, is not in use.

Stock netting: Galvanized wire mesh used as a stock-proof barrier.

Stock side: The side of the enclosure that faces the livestock.

Tamper: A tool used to compact soil and stone around a fencing post.

Tie ring: Small steel or galvanized ring, designed as an aid to tether equines, that can be affixed to walls.

Tongue-and-groove board: Used as an outer shell for buildings.

Top wire: Sometimes called 'single wire', and used to raise the height of stock fences. Used with post and rail, it can form a cost-effective equestrian boundary.